TOM CUNNINGHAM, BRAD SZOLLOSE AND JOHN WESTLEY CLAYTON PRESENT...

VOLUME 9

JOURNEYS TO SUCCESS

THE TOM CUNNINGHAM TRIBUTE EDITION

8 INTERNATIONAL AUTHORS SHARE THEIR **AMAZING STORIES OF RESILIENCE AND SUCCESS. BASED** ON **THE SUCCESS PRINCIPLES OF NAPOLEON HILL**

JOURNEYS
TO
SUCCESS

VOLUME 9

Tom 'too tall" Cunningham

Simply Amazing Edition

Publisher: John Westley Clayton

www.johnwestley.com

info@johnwestley.com

ISBN 978-1-947560-05-5

Table of Contents

Dedication

Very simply....

This book is dedicated to Tom "*too tall*" Cunningham.

June 19, 1963-April 9, 2018

Acknowledgements

There's only one person worthy of acknowledgment in this 9th edition of the Journeys To Success book series. That person would be the one and only Tom "*too tall*" Cunningham.

Tom was a certified Napoleon Hill Instructor, the creator of Journey To Success Radio and the Journeys To Success book series.

Thank you Tom for all that you've done for the world. Your "*AMAZING*" personal mental attitude, even while going through some incredible physical pain, helped more people than you could ever know.

Foreword

Lessons Learned from my husband, Tom Cunningham

Tom Cunningham gifted the people he loved around the world his lasting legacy -- his caring and support. Tom loved his family and always put those he loved first even before his own needs. Equally, Tom loved the Lord with all his heart and looked forward to going to heaven. Today, I know that Tom is there watching over and caring for all the lives he so intimately touch here on Earth for his 54 years. Tom stated, "*everyone has over 10,000 thoughts each day and we need to train ourselves to use these thoughts for positive outcomes. Negative thoughts are not welcome!*"

Tom conditioned himself to live positively through adversity. His mantra was "*Every day in every way I get better and better.*" During his most physically challenging times, this is exactly how he felt. When asked how he was doing, his signature reply was always "*AMAZING.*" He did this as a form of autosuggestion to himself when overcome with pain so as not to allow his mind to be influenced by his body. Truly, he was not feeling AMAZING, but he wanted to act as if he were. Tom encouraged people around the world by his positive modeling and through taking immediate action. His lasting legacy was and is his positive role modeling and purposeful self-conditioning for the benefit of others. He witnessed life as it was intended to be, not as he was experiencing it in his pain filled moments.

In his last moments, Tom smiled his amazing smile, spoke to his family and expressed love for all of us and tried to comfort me. He thanked his medical team for everything they had done for him. And he ended his life on his own terms by gifting us with one last memory of an amazing man, an amazing person, and a truly amazing model of an individual who endured his hardships daily for the benefit of his friends and family. Because of Tom's caring and charisma, he will continue to live on in our hearts and minds as each of us remember his positive, life-enhancing example.

Tom taught me the following life lessons:

1. Be thankful for what you have in all situations. Have an Attitude of Gratitude.
2. Know that there is always someone is in a worse situation than you are in right now.
3. Know that we are all children of God, and no better or no worse than anyone else.
4. Recognize the fact that you have been given life, and be appreciative of it.

Tom's website will remain active as his living legacy at www.tom2tall.com.

See you at the top, my Love!

Kim

Introduction

Superhuman. That is a word that Tom and I would use in our emails to give each other an extra little boost to our day. I loved opening up my inbox and seeing messages from tom2tall. I loved the authentic conversations that we had and I loved that we had a truth between each other that we did not have to explain.

Tom once wrote to me, "*You are a lifeline for me because you really know what I am experiencing.*"

Tom was a lifeline for me because he encouraged me to write about my experiences and share stories of adversity and show people the soft side of endurance and maintaining a never ending positive attitude no matter what our days present.

Our Positive Mental Attitude and our life long challenge of living with chronic illness was what wove our common cloth and it kept us connected. We both faced the daily fact that there was no medical cure to what ailments our body may encounter and the disease that hides underneath our skin was not in our control.

Control is such an interesting word. Of course, we can control what we put into our bodies and we can control the amount of exercise we do and we can control the environment that we surround ourselves in, but the reality still at the end of the day is there is no definite way to control the way our bodies react to "*our*" day at the end of that day.

For Tom and I, our bodies might give us some negative attitude, but our minds…that is (was) a different story. Our minds knew and challenged us each day to seek out our definite purpose and find all resources available to us to reach our common goal of making a difference in the lives of others by sharing our stories and giving people hope.

"When your desires are strong enough, you will appear to possess superhuman powers to achieve."

— Napoleon Hill

Tom and I met through the Napoleon Hill Foundation in the early Summer of 2014. He was always so positive in all of his messages. He had spoke to me many times about contributing to the Journeys to Success series but I always found a way (or excuse) not to dive into what I had told him I wanted to do – write, share and inspire.

Then the email came, Cyndi you have to do this one! We are naming it Positive Mental Attitude and that is what you are about! How do you find an excuse for that? You don't! You start writing. That first contribution has resulted in my tenure expanding over four books. Positive Mental Attitude, Journeys to Success Volume 6, 7 and 8, with each new writing allowing me to expand a breadth of personal and professional growth that can not be summed up quickly in this introduction. Tom knew that once I started writing I would not stop.

What can be expressed is my gratitude for having someone like Tom come into my life, a fellow spirit with a common cloth, to share my Journey. Our cloth is fashioned into a cape that shines with the letters of PMA along the back with the matching t-shirt logo across our chest and if you do not know what PMA stands for we will definitely take the time to show you, share with you and listen to your story as it is our major definite purpose.

I know that Tom continues to be a cheerleader for me and for all the contributing authors of this series. I would like to also express my gratitude to Brad Szollose and John Westley Clayton for assembling this tribute to our friend and colleague, and for continuing this legacy of Success. Together we are making a difference.

With much love,

Cyndi Vos, MEd

Positive Mental Attitude
The Fine Art of Parenting After Separation: The Power of a Positive Mental Attitude
Journey to Success, Health, Wellness & Fitness Edition, Volume 6
The Girl in the Red Bikini
Journey to Success, Volume 7
Johnny B
Journey to Success, Sales Professionals Edition, Volume 8

Bach, Beethoven, Brahms and Bartok: Lessons from the Big Four

***All Books received the stamp of International Bestseller**

CHAPTER 1

'Rock Bottom' Living without Hitting Rock Bottom

By Chuck Bolena M.Ed.

It is with great honor and a privilege to be part of this book series dedicated to Tom '*Too Tall*' Cunningham - an AMAZING friend, inspiring coach, and a passionate servant who blessed everyone he came in contact with. Tom, you have blessed me personally and demonstrated the power of faith and commitment to overcome any and all of life's obstacles. I am grateful for the time I spent with you as my coach, helping me become who I was meant to be and called to be – and, for that, I thank you.

I'm sitting in a Step-Down Unit room on the 5th floor of the Veteran's Hospital in Pittsburgh, Pennsylvania. It's late afternoon, the sun is shining and I can only assume it's warm outside as I look out and see the city building's light up from the setting sun as I begin writing this chapter. I am two days into a four to five-day stay following surgery to remove a section of my colon after being diagnosed with colon cancer. I admit I just started saying I was diagnosed with colon cancer instead of saying, "*they found cancer cells following a biopsy*." I'm guessing it was a verbal way to protect my mind from dreading the label. I will say, the care I've received at this VA Hospital has been 5-stars and the professionalism and courtesy of the staff – from the surgeons to the nurses, to Bill – the gentleman who cleans my room each morning and engages me in a discussion about our favorite airplanes and current events. This experience has been impeccable. Megan, Jenna, Kalyn, Katie, and Marty (my nurses) – thank you for your kindness, care, and patience with me so far during my stay. Father Sosa, thank you for the frequent conversations and special prayers when you visit. I am blessed.

From the onset of concern by the doctor over a large mass discovered during a random colonoscopy to the diagnosis of cancer and the surgery that followed to remove it, I have been at peace through it all. The kind of peace that transcends understanding and made me question myself a few times to be sure I truly understood the gravity of my situation. The only thing I can attribute this to is my faith and trust in my heavenly Father - a belief developed and influenced over my adult life. I do admit, my faith has waivered numerous times, but I do believe in and know my maker. Two of my key, spiritual mentors in my life, Jim Martin and Ron Jenkins - I thank you for demonstrating to me what a spirit-lead life looks like. In addition, the self-awareness and self-control that I've learned and developed over the last few years are from two great personal development mentors that I've come to know well: Jim Shorkey and Tom '*Too Tall*' Cunningham. These two have studied the teachings and writings of Napoleon Hill and many others, and have instilled in me the same sense of calm and coolness that each has mastered when one takes possession of their own mind and directs it to ends of their own choice. Without experiencing, first hand, how one can handle severe adversity in life, and demonstrate to me the learnable trait of self-control and mental focus, I believe I would have struggled far worse under my current predicament. I believe both the spiritual influence and the self-awareness are crucial for anyone to overcome all of life's struggles. The surgeon is confident with the outcomes of the surgery and I'm confident in them, so my mental focus is on that which I can control. I choose to seek the seed of an equal or greater opportunity in this adversity I'm faced with. What can I learn from this experience and how can God use it to bless those I interact with moving forward? I want to bless everyone I come in contact with and leave them with a sense of increase for having met me. This is my passion - my purpose.

[Jump ahead several weeks] So, I'm picking up where I left off; I am now out of the hospital. My three to five day stay turned into nine days total. I had an ileus following surgery that kept me from digesting foods or liquids and I would vomit everything I consumed. I was not given food or drink to allow my digestive system to heal and was only allowed ice chips to '*wet my whistle*.' I lost 15 pounds during my stay in the hospital and another two or three pounds after being released. I don't recall ever being hungry during my stay; it could have been due to the surgery, the medications, or simply an understanding that I had to endure it in order to get better. I will say that the prayers from friends and family during this time brought me comfort and '*fed me*' as I continued to stay focused and at peace. I will share, there was one point when I got really down and that was the day before I was released – the surgeon came in that morning and said I was doing well. He said, "*keep doing what you're doing and maybe we can talk about releasing you tomorrow*." He then turned and walked out of my room. Tomorow?! This conversation was at 6:00 in the morning. A day in the hospital seemed like forever and he told me "*maybe tomorrow!?*" I moped over that for hours before shaking it off. The next morning when he came in, he began telling me to keep doing what I was doing and we'll give it one more day. I was prepared this time and negotiated that I will attempt to eat food that day and, if successful, he can release me that afternoon. He said, "*you write the script and I'll sign it. But remember, if you can't keep food down you're back in here*." I said I understand and that I'll make him proud. The interns with him got a kick out of that and laughed! I felt really good and was determined to be released that day, and I was. My wife picked me up and the ride home was so enjoyable. I had the sunroof open and was like a little kid watching everything around me as if the scenery was new to me. As good as the hospital care was, I was happy to be going home. My dog, Gracey, freaked when she saw me and after running laps around the yard, stayed by my side like glue, making sure I didn't disappear again. She's my buddy!

On the day of my release, I was given my biopsy results from the surgery. The surgeon felt confident in the work he did, but the biopsy identified one lymph node outside the colon testing positive for cancer (which they did take out). Because of this, I'm labeled as having stage III colon cancer and scheduled to meet with oncology in the next few weeks for a consult about possibly going through chemo treatments. Again, I remain at peace with everything and will make decisions based on new information presented to me. No assumptions, worries or fears. Life is good and my journey continues!

I don't want to pretend that I haven't spent some time thinking of different scenarios that can come from this experience. I have given thought to the impact this will have on my wife, my kids, family and friends, my work, etc. Sure! I thought about it, but I did not let it '*get to me,*' if that makes sense. I don't like experiencing things blindly and thinking through it helps me better accept and process it. For one thing, I have a better appreciation for each day I wake. I am grateful for all that I have in my life and I speak gratitude to put myself in the best frame of mind as often as I can. I'm reevaluating my goals and making sure I'm chasing my true desires. I've developed an appreciation for the simple things in life: the warm sun on my face, a cool breeze, the taste of hot tea and honey, walking my dog or taking a nap!

I share this because, as I go through this hardship, I find that I'm learning more about myself and reevaluating life more. I just turned 49 and I did not predict a diagnosis of colon cancer, or any cancer, at any point in my life. Life events like this make you question the decisions you've made up to this point. I look back and think, am I living the life I had dreamed of or planned for at this stage in life? Do I have regrets? What can I do better today that I should have been doing all along? These are the questions that I get to answer and address for me and my life. I do find it interesting that I'm doing these things more intently now then I've ever done. They hold more significance and a sense of urgency now more than ever. I also find it interesting that I'm not the only one who goes through these life assessing emotions and thoughts when a hard reality sets in.

I have spent the last three years coaching clients through various life challenges and what I've seen is that many people need a 'rock-bottom experience' to alter their path in life. They allow difficulties and pains in life to continue so they can avoid facing their problems head-on; sometimes with circumstances, other times with people they love. They tolerate the pain and suffering and convince themselves that this is normal; that this is a part of life. They also believe they are the only ones suffering and often don't realize others in their lives are affected as well; again, no one says anything. They wait until their back is against the wall and there's no alternative but to face the truth; until their spouse says they're leaving because they don't feel loved any longer, or their boss tells them they're fired because they're not producing, or the doctor tells them they have a debilitating health issue because they failed to manage the stress and live a healthy lifestyle. It's interesting to see how attentive and alive people become at rock bottom. The natural abilities discovered to change course and do what should have been done all along are powerful. You read about it or see it on the news when an individual develops super-human strength to lift a car to help save someone in a crisis. They tap into a power that has always been within their capabilities. We all have that super-human talent to do things beyond what we believe we are capable of doing but rarely tap into it out of fear or lack of belief that it's possible.

Way too often most people are too comfortable and stay right where they are: unhappy, depressed, struggling to survive let alone truly live. About a year ago I sat in an emergency waiting room with a friend and across the room I watched a young woman (early 20s) argue with her father as she defended the boyfriend who beat her severely, which was the reason she's in there in the first place. Even though she is abused and mistreated frequently, she defends him and the situation she lives in because she knows what to expect, she finds comfort in the pain. I would also say, she either doesn't believe she is deserving of anything better or believes there is nothing better and fears life without him by her side. This is a common scenario and one that shows the human condition to stay with what's familiar and comforting instead of pushing through any fears, worries, and anxiety to improve one's situation. You've heard the simple story about how a frog will leap out of boiling water, but if you place him in water that's room temperature and slowly heat it, the frog will not leap out and will die in the boiling water. Too many people live life in the same way – not making changes unless something catastrophic takes place, and sometimes that's too late.

I've studied under Bob Proctor and he would always state that there are two ways in which people change in life: the first is by an emotional impact. This can be a loss of a loved one, experiencing a car crash, or being diagnosed with cancer. Emotional impacts are often negative and are not something that you can manifest easily. The second way is by repetition. By reinforcing again and again in one's mind a new positive belief to diminish a negative one that will create healthy change over time. One-way thrusts change upon you without choice, the other way is by choice and requires effort and discipline. Too many avoid the effort, never experience an emotional impact to force their hand, and never get a taste of what their life can really be like. They continue to live a life less than who they were meant to be. You see, "*God's gift to you is more talent and ability than you will ever use in one lifetime. Your gift to God is to develop and utilize as much of that talent and ability as you can, in this lifetime.*" I love this quote by Steve Bow.

Too many become too comfortable and never make the jump to experience life at the level that I believe they were meant to live. Dreams left behind, talents never manifested. We can never get lost time back.

Tom '*Too Tall*' Cunningham has demonstrated to me the power of stepping out and living the life he was meant to live. Against the odds of a debilitating chronic health condition that provided him every right to withdrawal and hide in constant pain, Tom stepped out and stepped up to help others overcome their life's struggles. He was a beacon of hope and possibility as he defeated the label of handicapped and lived his life as handicapable. He took to the stage and shared his faith, his resilience through difficult obstacles, and inspired thousands to see the power of thought and the influence you can have over your mind to achieve greatness. From his condo in Toronto, Tom would reach out to over 127 countries and impact the lives of people from all walks of life. They followed him on social media, they listened to his Journey to Success Podcast, they invited him to speak and he touched the hearts of those who listened. "***Amazing***" was Tom's mantra and he spoke it 99.999% of the time when you greeted him and asked how he was. Tom had every right to call it quits, but he persevered. He lived life to the fullest, using as much talent and abilities provided him by his maker. He demonstrated what happens when you let go and push forward. He leaves behind a legacy that has inspired many, many people to strive to live an Amazing life. The power of this one man demonstrates to me the power we all have inside us – we just need to tap into our talents and step up without fear.

I work as a mentor with my church's youth group and there is a young lady that lives with constant, chronic health issues that frequently lands her in the hospital for days on end. She is vibrant and filled with joy, but is frequently burdened with health issues that no young girl should worry about. Not long ago, I prayed with her at her request for health and family struggles, and afterward, I shared Tom's story with her. I told her he struggles with pain daily, but he chooses to greet people with the word '*Amazing*' and how it feeds him and blesses those who hear it. I challenged her to do the same; to answer others with the word 'Amazing' and to remember that it will alter her mindset positively as well as bless those she speaks it to. She said she would. I shared this with Tom through Facebook Messenger and this is his response I received on April 5th, 2018:

> *"Thank you for the prayers Chuck. I am finding it challenging to answer amazing however the reasons I give when people ask why remain the same. It seems like I have a medical appointment every day now and it never costs me $. Also, although I'm confined to our condo all day every day, it is a beautiful condo. I feel like I'm in prison much of the time but it is a very nice prison. Tell her to have a list of reasons why she is amazing because people will ask why. Every time she gives those reasons it will force her to think of her blessings. Remember that 4 out of 10 people in the world live on less than $2 per day and she is no nicer or more deserving to live in the U.S. than they are to live in a 3rd world country."*

Four days later, Tom '*Too Tall*' lost his fight here on earth, but I believe he is dancing in heaven, pain-free, and greets everyone he meets with the word "*Amazing*." His voice and positive outlook on life will forever resonate in my mind and the word '*Amazing*' will always remind me of the great man he was, and the strength and endurance he displayed against difficult odds. I aspire to walk the talk the way Tom has and intend to use his mantra often to bless others as well as encourage myself to keep on pushing forward.

Question for you, how are you living your life? Are you living the life you dreamed of twenty years earlier? Are you living with regrets? Are there circumstances in your life that need your attention and you're dragging your feet to avoid facing them head on? Does your life feel out of control? Does your life today look very similar to what it looked like a year ago? Are you growing, stagnant, or regressing? Be honest with yourself.

I pray your life is fulfilling and abundant with wonderful things to be grateful for. I challenge you to do some self-evaluation and give yourself the courage to address anything that is holding you back or tearing you down and to do so before you're forced to. Being diagnosed with diabetes or having a heart attack are not health issues suddenly thrust upon you. These conditions have taken some time, years in the making, to manifest to the point of attack. Muster the discipline and motivation to start handling the circumstances in your life that are holding your back now, and you will live a life without regrets. Free yourself from the shackles of mediocrity and the baggage you continue to drag along with you. It does not matter how difficult your life has been. Tomorrow's page is blank and you decide what goes on it for your life. Choose carefully!

Don't just exist, strive to feel alive, be ***Amazing*** and leave a legacy! You'll be glad you did.

One final note:

I want to recognize my wife, Darlene, who has demonstrated an incredible sense of courage and determination as she has stayed strong and supported me through my current health challenge. It's one thing for me to go through adversity personally, it's another thing to watch her watch me go through it. Her love and support has blessed me and motivated me to stay strong and to persevere. She is my beautiful bride, the love of my life, my partner in crime, and I love her very much. She makes this journey easier and more enjoyable by being by my side. *She's a **rockstar** and I love her.*

Chuck Bolena | Bio

Chuck is a Mindset Development Coach, Speaker, and Best Selling Author. He holds a Master's in Counseling and Development, Studied Mindset Mastery under Bob Proctor, and is a Certified John Maxwell Speaker, Trainer, and Leadership Coach. He has a long history of success, both in the US Air Force as a Nuclear Launch Officer, Instructor, and Evaluator, as well as in the pharmaceutical and medical device sales industry. He uses his skills, training, and personal experiences to nurture his passion for helping others overcome life's challenges. If you want to learn more about how Chuck can help you go after what you want in life, or would like to receive a complimentary discovery coaching session to uncover your true desires, he can be reached at chuck.bolena@resultsfromthinking.com

CHAPTER 2

The Unknown Dream

By Deana Mitchell

"Go confidently in the direction of your dreams,
live the life you have always imagined!"

— Henry David Thoreau

The seed was planted…

It was 1971 in Louisiana; I was about a year old when my dad decided to go back to school. My mom was trying to figure out how to work and not leave me in someone else's care. So out of necessity, she became an entrepreneur. She believed that necessity was the mother of invention, so she put her degree to work and opened a nursery school. That decision started her and our family on a journey that would last almost two decades. Being such a caring and giving person, my mom was and still is loved by everyone that knows her.

During my childhood, we would go to Plum Street Snowballs in New Orleans. A small family business for five generations, they had the best snowballs and usually a line around the block. I do realize that other than southerners, people call them snow cones! Little did I know; Plum Street would inspire my first business venture in 1984. My dad built a snowball stand in front of the nursery school, complete with a SnoWizard ice machine just like the one at Plum Street. The inventor that he is, he built all kinds of efficiencies inside for a smooth operation. Once it was complete he told me, "*if you need something, order it and if you don't feel like working, hire and train someone*." Being 14 at the time, I had no idea about business. That adventure taught me so much without this teenager even realizing it, my dad knew what he was doing. I had a captive audience of customers since it was positioned where parents picked up their kids each day, so it was relatively successful.

An unexpected adventure...

Finishing up my freshman year at Colorado State University in the spring or 1989, I received a call from my parents who stated they sold the nursery school, the house, the boat, my car and bought a motor home. At the time I was looking forward to going home and spending the summer with friends. They, along with my twelve-year-old brother picked me up in Fort Collins after the semester ended and we explored 33 states and 4 Canadian provinces that summer. Although my dad will tell you that I missed everything because I was a normal 19-year-old and just wanted to stay in the motor home and not be bothered, that only happened once. Yes, I missed seeing Mount St Helens because I wanted to be left alone... I was fascinated by many things on that trip, mostly the great outdoors, mountains, national parks and Telluride.

After that summer, I went back to school and ended up at Louisiana State University studying architecture. As one of three students in my class that had a full-time job, I rarely slept during those years. Many nights the three of us would be working in Atkinson Hall on projects that our classmates had finished during daylight hours. Luckily back then, we could have couches in our studio and I had friends who would wake me up for morning class. Every chance I got, I would design a restaurant or hotel because I was discovering that I was better at hospitality than architecture. I would work on efficient buildable designs and get Cs while my classmates were much more imaginative.

In the spring of 1990, a friend from CSU who lived in Alaska asked if I wanted to go work in Denali for the summer. I jumped at that opportunity and ended up working there in the summers of 1990 & 1992. The first year I worked as a housekeeper while realizing that the F&B employees made more money. So, when I went back in 1992, I had gained restaurant experience and became a server. Even though we worked full time, I spent every chance exploring the outdoors. That experience deepened my love of the mountains and I got hooked on white water rafting. I also fell in love with the sled dogs!

Climbing the hospitality corporate ladder…

During my years at LSU in Architecture I had several jobs, all of which were in the food and beverage industry. After receiving my degree, I continued in that industry moving several times to different states while climbing the corporate ladder. During this time, my dad repeatedly sent me prospects for architecture positions wondering why I was not interviewing for them. The hospitality industry treated me well for years and I was finding it hard to leave.

Around this time, due to downsizing and out of necessity, my dad stepped out on his own and started a successful business that is still alive today. He builds electrical and pneumatic panels for oilrigs, boats and electrical substations. Being that those panels must be labeled with engraved plastics, he also runs an engraving business.

I did leave the restaurant scene in the late nineties and started a second business venture that failed miserably. At that time, I just thought I needed to go back to hospitality because it was what I knew.

After several interviews, I started as a banquet manager in a New Orleans hotel. Not realizing how different restaurants and banquets were, I learned many valuable lessons the hard way. Determined to be successful, I poured my heart into my work. Although I loved my new endeavor, I was thinking about the mountains more and more.

In 1999 I moved to Snowmass Village, Colorado to be a Conference Services Manager for which I had no training. They interviewed me to be the Banquet Manager and then asked if I would consider Conference Services because unbeknownst to me at the time, they were losing most of the department. So, the first winter season, it was myself and one other person from the Front Desk. I taught her how to write menus and she taught me about reservations and we made it through! By the end of the season, we were both self-taught Delphi experts!

"Just tell me I cannot do something, and I will prove you wrong"

— Deana Mitchell

Working more than normal hours, I still found time to learn to ski and I was in love! Back then I looked like the out of town guest with the less than hip gear. I also went through training to be a white-water raft guide. I was in heaven and never thought I would ever leave that town. Snowmass will always have a place in my heart!

It was October 2000 and we were all preparing for a busy winter season, when the Banquet Manager did not show up for work. The management asked me to step in and help run the department, but we were also minus a boss in Conference Services. Until March, I ran the banquet department in addition to my primary duties. I worked a ton of hours that season, but we had an amazing banquet team and the clients were happy.

More unexpected adventures...

At the end of that ski season, because of the extra work and pay, I took a solo month-long trip. I visited Tahiti, New Zealand and Australia. Amazing opportunity and I learned quite a bit about myself that year.

That fall, I climbed my first fourteener, Handies Peak. This is what Coloradoans call the 54 mountains that are 14,000' or higher. No thanks to my friends, I was not at all prepared for climbing that first one. They just assumed I knew what I was getting into, but I had no idea. It was just a couple of weeks after 9/11 and we took pictures at the summit with an American Flag, it was a huge accomplishment for me and I was hooked.

The move that changed my life...

After another ski season, I was ready for a new challenge and moved to Georgia for a job opportunity. I really did not want to leave Colorado, but I just felt like it was the right decision for some reason. Since I had never been able to have pets in Snowmass housing, I adopted a retired husky sled dog named Muggs. He was 12 and in perfect shape from being a lead dog his whole life. In Georgia, I adopted another husky named Nala. She was smart and about 18 months old at the time. Then I figured out why God had me leave Colorado, I met the love of my life who was a fellow manager at the resort where I was working. When we started talking outside of work, I told him although the South was home, I was planning to go back to Colorado at some point. He agreed that he would like to move West and we were married about a year later.

About 18 months later we moved to Colorado and both worked at the same resort in Vail for about 5 years. Muggs died in the middle of that time and I was devastated, but he had a great retirement and lived to be seventeen. Towards the end of that stint, the recession and housing crash hit, and my husband was sent on task force opportunities around the US and was away from home for months.

Back to Telluride...

That is when it happened, my husband accepted a

new job and I got to go back to Telluride... 21 years after my first visit in the family motor home. It really is the most beautiful place I have lived, and we were excited for a new adventure.

Now I had to figure out what I was going to do and after a few months I decided out of necessity, I would become an entrepreneur much like my mom did almost 40 years prior. Although I still didn't use my degree, I capitalized on the decades of experience in the hospitality world.

Little did we know at the time; my husband's new job would send him even further away and for longer periods of time. During the next five years he would be traveling more than he was home. He spent seven months in Doha, Qatar in 2012 and we also split our time between Telluride and Aspen for a couple years.

Realizing the Unknown Dream...

Once I made the decision to start a business, I had a very clear picture of the future and it was somewhat surreal. From that time on I was driven by determination, but most of all faith. The first two years, I had a full-time job and put half my check into the business. The objective from the beginning was to be a DMC and work with corporate and incentive groups, but the first three years I planned and executed about 50 weddings mostly in Telluride. I worked with some corporate clients during those first years, but I was determined to make that the focus.

After losing Nala, I was sitting at my desk on a quiet day in August of 2014 and I received an email that changed everything. A month later Realize Colorado was officially a Global DMC Partner! Soon after I made the decision to quit taking wedding business. Since that time, we have grown astronomically and opened a second office in 2016, Denver.

The principles that guided me…

Most of these principles I learned as a kid, not from Napoleon Hill but from my parents who were full of integrity and good morals. That does not mean I fully understood them all at the time but have applied the knowledge throughout my life. Growing with every hard-learned lesson, and there have been more than I can count, has made me a better person in a thousand ways.

"Every adversity, every failure, every heartbreak, carries with it the seed of an equivalent or greater benefit"

— Napoleon Hill

I am a believer of the saying, "*everything happens for a reason*", and that means the good and the bad.

The burning desire for achievement and success has always lived in me. I am extremely competitive, which was a planted seed at an early age by my dad. Our family played every game you can imagine in our free time. Dad always won, but I finally beat him at Monopoly when I was in college! He was good at anything he ever did, I am blessed that maybe a little of that rubbed off on me.

Once Realize was born, I felt that burning desire more than ever. Out of all the employers I had worked for, I never wanted to let them down in any way. Now more than ever, I did not want to let myself down.

"He had nothing to start with, except the capacity to know what he wanted, and the determination to stand by that desire until he realized it "

— Napoleon Hill

Deeply inspired by the mountains and rivers around me, I planned to grow this new business. It took lots of personal initiative and self-discipline. I know the old cliché that 'being your own boss' is the greatest thing ever, but if you are not motivated it is impossible. There is no one to tell you when to show up or how to be successful, it is all on you to figure it out.

"Self-discipline begins with the mastery of thought. If you do not control your thoughts, you cannot control your needs. Self-discipline calls for a balancing of the emotions of your heart with the reasoning faculty of your head."

— Napoleon Hill

Half the battle is keeping your thoughts positive and yourself motivated. Surround yourself by successful people and constantly be reading and learning from people who have already become successful. Developing positive habits to keep you in that motivated mindset can be a life changer. The more you speak about what you want to happen, the more you will realize your dream.

"Whatever the mind can conceive and believe, it can achieve"

— Napoleon Hill

Going the extra mile is a principle that I have always taken a bit to the extreme. Thirty-minute meetings would turn into three hours because I wanted to help with things for which I was not compensated. On the other hand, it made me feel good and it helped me build great relationships with people. For instance, one bride I worked with ended up years later introducing me in a round about way to someone who is now one of my best team members. You never know how relationships will develop over time and what a person you just met will mean to you in the long run. On the other hand, time management is invaluable to anyone trying to build a successful business. I never thought I had enough time, and still need forty hours in a day!

Our company is based on ideas. Creativity is the basis of all that we do in our business. You must possess something creative that a client has not already done to bring the most value and win their trust. We spend time and money on that exact concept. How can we be better? How can we make the next event for XYZ client better than the last? Imagination is key!

"Creative vision is developed by the free and fearless use of one's imagination."

— Napoleon Hill

"The way of success is the way of continuous pursuit of knowledge"

—Napoleon Hill

Once you can harness the creativity and imagination, you need controlled attention to put it to work and make the most of your ideas. Logistics and details are necessary to bring your creativity to life. Persistence and determination are always needed to stay the course and get to the finished product.

"Set your mind on a definite goal and observe how quickly the world stands aside to let you pass."

—Napoleon Hill

The above quote is reality more than you can imagine. If you possess the passion, confidence and determination for what you are trying to accomplish, and you prove yourself even in small ways, you will be surprised how people will rally to your aid and help make it happen. I have been amazed by the support I have received from friends and colleagues, but even more by people who did not even know me. The original tagline and logo for my business was "*Realize what you Imagine*". It has also been my mantra since the beginning. I was in awe of the plan greater than me that allowed all my experiences in life to culminate in this beautiful place that I never knew I would see again, Telluride. It also answered my question of why I had moved so much and done so many different things, all experience needed to run a business like the one I started out of necessity. One of my early employees said to me, "*you are always thinking about the future and what is next*". After thinking about it, I agreed with her and realized myself that I was speaking what I wanted, and it would happen.

The quote below holds some truth in my case as I started my business at 40 and I am looking forward to what happens after 50!

"Those who succeed in an outstanding way seldom do so before the age of 40. More often, they do not strike their real pace until they are well beyond the age of 50"

—Napoleon Hill

The journey has had its share of adversity & defeat. In the early years there were clients that did not chose to work with me and the worst part was not understanding why. Some bad financial decisions caused un-needed strife. There were people or companies I wanted to partner with that did not reciprocate. Being in a business where most people do not understand what you do makes it difficult all around. I have worked with clients who had never hired a DMC because they did not understand that we could act as a partner and extension of their team. Once they worked with us, they said they will never do another event without a DMC. It is all about understanding the objectives and working as a team to reach a goal.

"Individual success usually is in exact proportion of the scope of the defeat the individual has experienced and mastered. Many so-called failures represent only a temporary defeat that may prove to be a blessing in disguise."

—Napoleon Hill

"Teamwork is harmonious cooperation that is willing, voluntary and free. Whenever the spirit of teamwork is the dominating influence in business or industry, success is inevitable. Harmonious cooperation is a priceless asset that you can acquire in proportion to your giving."

— Napoleon Hill

Our current team is the definition of teamwork and I am super proud of each of them individually. We have accomplished so much in a short time and it is only possible because we work together towards our goals and support each other daily.

And the greatest of these is love...

Faith, hope, love but also humility and kindness are what drives me as a person. My dad's constant message to me in my adult life has been, "*God has a plan for your life*". It has taken me decades to fully understand and believe that, but I do believe it to my core. I was blessed to have unconditional love and support from my family growing up. And the fact that I was told I could do or be anything I wanted, gave me confidence in my abilities.

I grew up in the church, but never had a deep understanding or personal relationship with my Savior until I was in my thirties. After a rough emotional time, I turned back to my faith and since then it has been stronger than ever. I feel that Jesus Christ is a lamp to my feet and he guides me in everything. In those tough times when I was not sure my business would continue, my faith got me through and there was a plan greater than I imagined.

"Most great people have achieved their greatest success just one step beyond their greatest failure"

— Napoleon Hill

"Faith rather than fear, freedom rather than failure"

— Brian Biro

History has repeated itself a few times in my family. My mom, dad, and brother all began successful businesses from nothing, so I had the benefit of learning from them. I have been blessed with a certain level of success, but it is due to persistence, determination and most of all a ton of faith!

My husband has been more loving and supportive than I could ask for from any human being. He amazes me daily with his consistency and faith. I would truly not be the person I am today without him.

How many of you have had a dream that you never acknowledged or even knew was there? Wishing that you too will find your passion and realize your dream.

Unfortunately, I never had the pleasure of meeting Tom "*too tall*" Cunningham, but he did touch my life in a profound way. When I first read about Tom, I watched a video of his testimony and was amazed by the amount of pain he had dealt with in his life while keeping such an AMAZING attitude! During the last eight years, I too have dealt with health issues, but nothing like Tom. Hearing his testimony gave me a very different outlook on not feeling well and still being AMAZING all the time!

Deana Mitchell , CMP DMCP CCSE | Bio

Deana Mitchell is the Owner & Founder of Realize Colorado, a Global DMC Partner. Realize is a Destination Management company that serves the great state of Colorado.

Deana's background includes almost three decades in the hospitality industry with proven successful results in the planning and execution of all kinds of events. The first 10 years of her career were spent in restaurant and banquet management, and then proceeded on to conference, catering, and destination services. In 2005, Deana earned the Certified Meeting Professional designation, in 2012 earned the Destination Management Certified Professional designation and in 2015 earned the Customer Certified Sales Expert designation.

Deana has visited 49 states and resided in eight of them. Colorado is absolutely her favorite to live and work. She should know as she has lived and worked in seven different Colorado cities!

She has realized her dream of living in the mountains and enjoying life every day! Her experience in the different facets of the hospitality world over the years, coupled with her travels and involvement in professional organizations, gives her the ideal experience to do what she loves – creating experiences for groups who want to visit Colorful Colorado!

Currently serves on the Destination Colorado Board & the Global DMC Partners DMC Advisory Board.

Realize Colorado is the 2017 US Partner of the Year awarded by Global DMC Partners.

www.realizecolorado.com

deana@realizecolorado.com

https://www.linkedin.com/in/deanamitchell/

CHAPTER 3

Striving for an Ultimate Goal

By Geoff Hudson-Searle

"Fame is part of me and my life as an actor. I enjoy the creative aspects of my life as an actor. I enjoy directing and acting as well. But the bottom line for me is not prestige and power. It's about having an exciting, creative life."

— Matt Dillon

What is Prestige

What is Prestige in our now world. The Oxford dictionary has its definition as: "*prestige, /prɛˈstiː(d)ʒ/, noun: prestige; widespread respect and admiration felt for someone or something on the basis of a perception of their achievements or quality.*"

Each of us is, to some extent or other, a reflection of the experiences of our lives. However, whether and how we succeed is determined at least in part by how we cope with those experiences and what we learn from them. Everyone has a story, despite difficulties in family life and professional setbacks, the journey to success is the learnings we all have, we all possess the determination, drive and skills to create a successful and happy life, the bigger question is if we choose to use these skills.....for the great of good.

Recently, I sat in an Italian coffee house on the South Bank of the Thames in London – United Kingdom, I thought about those years. Experiencing the highest of highs and the lowest of lows, and I knew that I had been tested in ways that I could never of expected. And yet, I had prevailed. Despite the frustration, anger and fear, I had created a company that fulfilled the vision, I had kept a company alive against all odds, and I had moved it to a point where it was thriving.

I also had learned a lot about myself. I had been forced to recognize my own weaknesses and eccentricities, and I had discovered reserves of strength that I had not known I had. In the process, I had become less judgmental and more accepting of myself and of others.

I realized that leadership forces you to stay true to yourself and to recognize when you are at your best and when you are at your worst; the important thing is to stay focused and keep moving forward. I learned that it is overcoming adversity that brings the most satisfaction, and that achievements are made more meaningful by the struggle it took to achieve them.

I had felt that learning through the ups and downs of my personal and professional life that anything is possible if you believe in yourself and if you set your mind and heart to it. If you want something badly enough, you must be prepared to go after it with everything you have, no matter what the consequences.

The important thing is to decide what you really want. Having time out, I was able to envision a different kind of company, one in which there were shared values and shared dreams. Although there were problems to be solved along the way, I persevered and created that company.

I had the very fortune of learning more about myself by being put into adverse circumstances than I could ever have learned about myself from a psychometric test or a new Oxford business book; it was reserves of inner self and energy that made the journey possible.

Change has a funny habit of teaching you much about yourself; it goes to the core of your own weaknesses, strengths and eccentricities. Leadership forces you to stay true to yourself and recognize times when you are at your best and worst; the key is to stay focused and to make decisions that will look at continuous improvement. Even though this may be small, incremental change, it is positive change you can build upon even though you may be in quicksand.

Business has taught me much about life, learning and sharing knowledge and life stories with my employees and associates. My hopes, fears, beliefs, values and dreams were tested to the limit. I learned that only the difficult things in life truly bring satisfaction, and that achievement is proportional to the struggle needed to get there.

I had no idea what the future might hold, but I was glad that I had followed my dreams. I have often reminisced sipping my favourite coffee, recalling the words of Winston Churchill: "*This is not the end. It is not even the beginning of the end. But it is, perhaps, the end of the beginning.*"

Prestige or Purpose – this is the question?

"I've learned that making a living is not the same thing as making a life"

— Maya Angelou

Chad Albrecht from the Huntsman School of Business wrote an article on productivity and prestige in business ethics research. Based on a survey that was administered to 320 business ethics scholars worldwide, the authors report a ranking of 15 business schools that are perceived to be leaders in the field of business ethics. Based on these same survey results, the authors investigated which factors may have the strongest relationship to individual publication productivity and perceptions of institutional prestige within business ethics research. The results provided several surprising findings that suggest the business ethics field may be anomalous in academe in terms of the emergence of productivity and prestige.

Efficiency at doing a certain task, in the workplace or otherwise, is strongly influenced by how motivated individuals are. Exploring new ways to motivate employees is often at the top of a company's agenda. Traditionally identified motivators in Western economies primarily include salary and prestige, often complemented by meaning, creation, challenge, ownership and identity.

Whether in our private or professional life, every day we complete a certain number of tasks, some of which are more or less pleasurable to do. Of course, when motivated or stimulated to do certain tasks, we often complete them faster, better and without procrastination, even when the tasks themselves are not very pleasurable. Motivation in general comes from a wide range of personal or social factors, such as financial compensation (salary), recognition by the colleagues or superiors (prestige), or satisfaction coming from personal achievements. It comes as no surprise that employers and companies are systematically seeking new ways to stimulate their employees towards being more productive and happier at the same time. In conditions of radical social and cultural changes, in particular those related to the emerging knowledge economy, enterprises are facing new challenges to motivate and retain key workforce, which is the focus factor of competitiveness in the market.

So, while perceived prestige in the industry continues to be an important factor, it seems that priorities have certainly shifted in the marketplace, and people today are most concerned now with finding a workplace that suits their lifestyle and personality.

It really does not matter what is motivating you but the fact that you recognize it. It is exhausting to deny your true motivations. If you are motivated by money, growth, possessions, your family, partner and friends – that's great. Accept it. Run with it. Maximize those desires. Work hard, get paid, do it again. When you harness your motivations, you can achieve a lot. It's a source of energy and gives your work purpose.

But ask the question frequently, "*What's motivating me right now?*" Your motivations change on a regular basis. At some points you will be motivated by the work, and at others you will want the kudos and applause. Whatever it is, pay, prestige or process, embrace the motivation at that moment. Let it fuel your passion, your prestige may well become the motivational factor and energy behind your purpose.

Writing is another channel has really changed my life. I have always believed that it is your right to speak truthfully in all matters that concern you and to speak from the heart.

It has been an overwhelming experience to receive emails and phone calls from people across all walks of life wanting to share their experiences, their story. Entrepreneurs, business people, students, children, and charitable causes have approached me for keynote sessions, general advice, and inspiration leadership.

I have been overwhelmed with inquiries but will continue to expand and express the journey that each and every one of us deserves, within our heart-motivated purpose in life, because there is a 'journey to success.'

Every audience has a different dynamic, a different rhythm, and a different reaction. The audience wants, needs, and expects pertinent, real-life information to enrich and support their lives and importantly what they're facing. I believe it was my destiny in life to push things to the limit. You only get one chance to make an impression. I gave 'Freedom After the Sharks' and '*Meaningful Conversations*' every opportunity I had of the events that took place for what I believed to be right and true.

In life you survive. You move on but with a purpose. A great philosopher and friend in the US once told me 'that you are in this world by divine right and you have the right to reach your highest potential through your own uniqueness'. I know so many people who are only in bliss when they are miserable. They blame their parents, their spouse, their family, the system, their employers, their friends for their individual failings.

You know what's amazing — and I've said this for years — you have the capacity to love and be loved with an open heart. You can do whatever you have to do to get past your problem; you can do it. The question is how much you want the dream or the purpose.

It's your quiet inner drive and tenacious disciplined focus that will set yourself apart from those who seemingly fall by the way side. This may sound a little strange but when I'm asked about the key to my journey to success, it has always been that guttural ignorant persistence. You do more, you give a little more of yourself in everything you do until it becomes a natural part of your lifestyle, it is also important to be a mentor to those who need help, encouragement and share.

I believe we know enough now to see which strategies will increase productivity, emotional and human engagement, and strategic planning and development for life and growth.

As social beings, we want to trust each other, our character and our integrity.

The speed of the Internet, technology and importantly how people behave on the Internet can be a constant treadmill. Consider the proportion of people who say that other people can be trusted, the proportion who belong to social organizations, the divorce rate, the unemployment rate, the quality of government, and religious belief. Unfortunately, over the last 50 years levels of trust have fallen drastically in the United Kingdom and the United States of America, though not in continental Europe. In the United States and Britain, the percentage of adults who think that most people can be trusted is half that of the 1950s. Policies that encourage trust are thus extremely important; these include moral education in schools, and policies to build stable families, communities and workplaces.

Why H2H and a sense of purpose is still what real people focus upon

By now you've probably heard a lot about wearables, living services, the 'Internet of Things' and smart materials. As designers working in these realms, we've begun to think about even weirder and wilder things, envisioning a future where evolved technology is embedded inside our digestive tracts, sense organs, blood vessels, and even our cells.

Let's talk about a scourge of modern times. There is so much stuff to watch, read, listen to, buy, eat or learn about. The world is available at our fingertips at any moment. It feels glorious but also horribly, paralyzingly overwhelming.

Should I wade into Spotify's sea of every song ever recorded or give up and listen to my downloaded copy of Beyonce's "*Crazy for Love*" for the 47,000th time? Psychologist Barry Schwartz called this the "*Paradox of choice*" in his 2004 book of the same name. Like many ideas that come out of TED Talks, it is too simplistic to say more choices are counterproductive, but I think we've all experienced the feeling.

Naturally, technology companies have some ideas about how to help people discover things and select among the flood of options — and make money in the process. And even they are recognizing the limits of technology in helping people stay informed and entertained.

To see the future, first we must understand the past. Humans have been interfacing with machines for thousands of years. We seem to be intrinsically built to desire this communion with the made world. This blending of the mechanical and biological has often been described as a "*natural*" evolutionary process by such great thinkers as Marshall McLuhan in the '50s and more recently Kevin Kelly in his seminal book What Technology Wants. So, by looking at the long timeline of computer design we can see waves of change and future ripples.

The effects of technological change on the global economic structure are creating immense transformations in the way companies and nations organize production, trade goods, invest capital, and develop new products and processes. Sophisticated information technologies permit instantaneous communication among the far-flung operations of global enterprises. New materials are revolutionizing sectors as diverse as construction and communications. Advanced manufacturing technologies have altered long-standing patterns of productivity and employment. Improved air and sea transportation has greatly accelerated the worldwide flow of people and goods.

All this has both created and mandated greater interdependence among firms and nations. The rapid rate of innovation and the dynamics of technology flows mean that comparative advantage is short-lived. To maximize returns, arrangements such as transnational mergers and shared production agreements are sought to bring together partners with complementary interests and strengths. This permits both developed and developing countries to harness technology more efficiently, with the expectation of creating higher standards of living for all involved.

Rapid technological innovation and the proliferation of transnational organizations are driving the formation of a global economy that sometimes conflicts with nationalistic concerns about maintaining comparative advantage and competitiveness. It is indeed a time of transition for firms and governments alike.

In the markets of the United Kingdom and the United States, we are constantly seeing '*flexibility*' and '*change*' to our economies; this evidence is continuing with the '*Gig Economy*,' the millennials and a new operating business economy. There are huge advantages to inflexibility and predictability, as continental Europeans appreciate. The evidence shows that continuous re-optimization is not always the best route to building solid, sustainable foundations for business and relationships.

People also want to be trusted and respected themselves. This requires that they have some responsibility and autonomy. Most of us like to feel we are working well or helping others, because we could not expect to be respected otherwise. That is a key element in the motivation to work, the satisfaction of the professional norm. Yet in recent years employers have used more and more financial incentives to motivate people: Performance-related pay has been creeping in everywhere, including the public service.

With all of these considerations, are mainstream economists right or wrong in how they approach our social and economic problems? Partly right, partly wrong. Here is the good part: Each individual knows more about himself or herself than anyone else does.

So, there are huge gains all round if we can freely exchange goods and services with each other, including our labour. This is especially so where markets are large and well informed and no one affects anyone else except through the process of voluntary exchange. Indeed, economists have correctly shown that if these conditions exist and contracts can be enforced and people can start sharing within a '*shared economy,*' the outcome will be fully '*efficient*.' In other words, everyone will be happy as is possible without someone else being less happy. This important claim helps to explain the extraordinary success of post-war capitalism in producing material advance.

Yet, why did this advance not guarantee a rise in personal happiness? The reason is that many of the most important things that touch us do not reach us through voluntary exchange. Nor have our tastes, expectations and norms remained unchanged, and these too affect our happiness.

Values in people can also change. In the last 50 years we have become increasingly independent and individualistic. We are ever more influenced by the Internet and versions of the '*survival of the fittest;*' Charles Darwin said, '*It is not the strongest of the species that survives, nor the most intelligent that survives. It is the one that is most adaptable to change*.' Describing '*the invisible hand,*' Adam Smith said: 'The great source of both the misery and disorders of human life, seems to arise from over-rating the difference between one permanent situation and another. Avarice over-rates the difference between poverty and riches: ambition, that between a private and a public station: vain-glory, that between obscurity and extensive reputation.'

The person under the influence of any of those extravagant passions, is not only miserable in his actual situation, but is often disposed to disturb the peace of society, in order to arrive at that which he so foolishly admires. The slightest observation, however, might satisfy him, that, in all the ordinary situations of human life, a well-disposed mind may be equally calm, equally cheerful, and equally contented. Some of those situations may, no doubt, deserve to be preferred to others: but none of them can deserve to be pursued with that passionate ardour, which drives us to violate the rules either of prudence or of justice; or to corrupt the future tranquillity of our minds, either by shame from the remembrance of our own folly, or by remorse from the horror of our own injustice.'

The true values of Human 2 Human

My final thought in the matter is that the answer to technological overload is not less technology but more humanity.

Digital transformation, solving problems with technology, exponential growth through technology, the integration of humans/machines, Artificial Intelligence, Internet of Things etc. Like it or not, there is no way out, technology has taken over already: I lived without a Smartphone for a few weeks to find out that you soon get excluded from communities, groups, discussions and business.

The problem is not development of new technology; this is nothing new for humanity. The problem is the speed and the major impact it creates for us. It is paradoxical, but humans have the capacity to create innovation and technology with which, at the same time, they have problems keeping up with, technically, emotionally and as a society. We are used to slow, incremental change. Only few people can keep up with the speed and nature of change, most of us get anxious and try to row backwards.

The most important things for our survival are not digital: air, water, food, clothes, emotions, the warmth of a human body next to us. Spending time with people living in a strong connection with and in and from nature was eye opening: we do not live in and with the nature, we are a part of nature, fully integrated with it.

We should ask: "*If technology was supposed to make our lives easier and better, why is everybody so exhausted?*". "*How can we stay present and awake in a world of distraction and consumption?*"

My belief is that a society cannot flourish without some sense of shared purpose. The current pursuit of self-realization will not work. If your sole duty is to achieve the best for yourself, life becomes just too stressful and too isolated and lonely, and you will be set up to fail. Instead, you need to feel you exist for something larger, and that very thought takes off some of the pressure.

We desperately need a concept of a common purpose, a common vision and a sense of working together to achieve the one overall goal. Human happiness comes from the outside and from within. The two are not in contradiction. The secret is compassion towards oneself and others, and the principle of the greatest happiness is essentially the expression that can all share connections. Perhaps these are the cornerstones of our future culture.

I believe now is the moment to define our terms. Technology is fast, and fast is getting faster, fast is busy, controlling, aggressive, hurried, analytical, stressed, superficial, impatient, active, quantity-over-quality. Slow is the opposite: calm, careful, receptive, still, intuitive, unhurried, patient, reflective, quality-over-quantity. It is about making real and meaningful connections – with people not machines, culture, work, food, everything.

We do not want high turnover in jobs, in housing or in marriages, except where clear advantages outweigh the human and other costs. Nor do we want our firms and public services to be repeatedly restructured, with massive loss of trust at every stage.

In the markets of the United Kingdom and the United States, we are constantly seeing 'flexibility' and 'change' to our economies; this evidence is continuing with the '*Gig Economy*,' the millennials and a new operating business economy. There are huge advantages to inflexibility and predictability, as continental Europeans appreciate. The evidence shows that continuous re-optimisation is not always the best route to building solid, sustainable foundations for business and relationships.

People also want to be trusted and respected themselves. This requires that they have some responsibility and autonomy. Most of us like to feel we are working well or helping others, because we could not expect to be respected otherwise. That is a key element in the motivation to work, the satisfaction of the professional norm. Yet in recent years employers have used more and more financial incentives to motivate people: Performance-related pay has been creeping in everywhere, including the public service.

With all of these considerations, are mainstream economists right or wrong in how they approach our social and economic problems? Partly right, partly wrong. Here is the good part: Each individual knows more about himself or herself than anyone else does. So, there are huge gains all round if we can freely exchange goods and services with each other, including our labour. This is especially so where markets are large and well informed and no one affects anyone else except through the process of voluntary exchange. Indeed, economists have correctly shown that if these conditions exist and contracts can be enforced and people can start sharing within a 'shared economy,' the outcome will be fully 'efficient.' In other words, everyone will be happy as is possible without someone else being less happy. This important claim helps to explain the extraordinary success of post-war capitalism in producing material advance.

Yet why did this advance not guarantee a rise in personal happiness? The reason is that many of the most important things that touch us do not reach us through voluntary exchange. Nor have our tastes, expectations and norms remained unchanged, and these too affect our happiness.

Values in people can also change. In the last 50 years we have become increasingly independent and individualistic. We are ever more influenced by the Internet and versions of the '*survival of the fittest;*' describing '*the invisible hand,*' Adam Smith said: '*The great source of both the misery and disorders of human life, seems to arise from over-rating the difference between one permanent situation and another. Avarice over-rates the difference between poverty and riches: ambition, that between a private and a public station: vain-glory, that between obscurity and extensive reputation. The person under the influence of any of those extravagant passions, is not only miserable in his actual situation, but is often disposed to disturb the peace of society, in order to arrive at that which he so foolishly admires. The slightest observation, however, might satisfy him, that, in all the ordinary situations of human life, a well-disposed mind may be equally calm, equally cheerful, and equally contented. Some of those situations may, no doubt, deserve to be preferred to others: but none of them can deserve to be pursued with that passionate ardour which drives us to violate the rules either of prudence or of justice; or to corrupt the future tranquillity of our minds, either by shame from the remembrance of our own folly, or by remorse from the horror of our own injustice*.'

We desperately need a concept of a common purpose, a common vision and a sense of working together to achieve the one overall goal. Human happiness comes from the outside and from within. The two are not in contradiction. The secret is compassion towards oneself and others, and the principle of the greatest happiness is essentially the expression that can all share connections. Perhaps these are the cornerstones of our future culture.

I believe now is the moment to define our terms. Fast is busy, controlling, aggressive, hurried, analytical, stressed, superficial, impatient, active, quantity-over-quality. Slow is the opposite: calm, careful, receptive, still, intuitive, unhurried, patient, reflective, quality-over-quantity. It is about making real and meaningful connections - with people, culture, work, food, everything

From 'Your Forces and How to Use Them,' by Christian D. Larson

Promise Yourself

To be so strong that nothing can disturb your peace of mind.

To talk health, happiness, and prosperity to every person you meet.

To make all your friends feel that there is something in them

To look at the sunny side of everything and make your optimism come true.

To think only the best, to work only for the best, and to expect only the best.

To be just as enthusiastic about the success of others as you are about your own.

To forget the mistakes of the past and press on to the greater achievements of the future.

To wear a cheerful countenance at all times and give every living creature you meet a smile.

To give so much time to the improvement of yourself that you have no time to criticize others.

To be too large for worry, too noble for anger, too strong for fear, and too happy to permit the presence of trouble.

To think well of yourself and to proclaim this fact to the world, not in loud words but great deeds.

To live in faith that the whole world is on your side so long as you are true to the best that is in you.

Final thought

My final thought in the matter is that a society cannot flourish without some sense of shared purpose. The current pursuit of self-realisation will not work. If your sole duty is to achieve the best for yourself, life becomes just too stressful and too lonely, and you will be set up to fail. Instead, you need to feel you exist for something larger, and that very thought takes off some of the pressure.

'*find something more important than you are,*' philosopher Dan Dennett once said in discussing the secret of happiness, '*and dedicate your life to it.*' But how, exactly, do we find that? Surely, it isn't by luck. I myself am a firm believer in the power of curiosity and choice as the engine of fulfilment, but precisely how you arrive at your true calling is an intricate and highly individual dance of discovery. Still, there are certain factors and certain choices on your journey to success that make it easier and more worthwhile......

The question is, how much do you truly want your dream and do you have the courage to pursue it?

Geoff Hudson-Searle | Bio

Geoff is an international commercial director, Non-Executive Director, CMO, CEO and strategist, lecturing regularly on the principles of integrated strategy at worldwide forums, rated by Agilience as a Top 250 Harvard Business School authority, covering strategic management and management consulting, and has over 25 years of experience in the business and management arena, an author of his first book *'Freedom after the Sharks' and recently 'Meaningful Conversations*'. A member and fellow of the Institute of Directors, associate of The Business Institute of Management and a co-founder and board member of the Neustar International Security Council (NISC). He holds a Masters degree in Business Administration. Having worked for corporate companies Citibank N.A, MICE Group Plc, Enigma Design, MMT Inc, Kaspersky Laboratory, Bartercard Plc, and RG Group around the world, Geoff has vast international experience working with SME and International clients. International clients with which Geoff has worked include the British Government, HP, Compaq, BT, Powergen, Intel, ARM, Watsila Group, Atari, Barclays Bank, Societe Generale, Western Union, Chase and Volvo. Geoff has worked in a broad range of industries including software, technology and banking which has given him a range of different experiences and perspectives of what can work, the importance of good people, process and how these can be applied and amplified to deliver results in different scenarios and paradigms. Geoff is known for bringing in a fresh and sometimes challenging the status-quo, with a strategic approach delivering successful change management programmes and launching companies and products internationally that deliver results. For example he once started with a company carrying a loss of £15M, and responsible for executing a new 24 month plan for generating £60M of solution sales revenue across 12 countries in EMEA. Geoff's areas of expertise lie in brand strategy, business communications, business integration, business development and improvement, capital raise activities, pre-IPO planning, capital raise transactions, M&A with full P&L responsibility, which ideally equips him to strengthen global companies, develop SME and international business, and marketing strategies.

Contact information:

Geoffrey Hudson-Searle

Email: ghudsonsearle@gmail.com

Tel: +44 (0) 207 205 2490

Linkedin: http://www.linkedin.com/in/geoffsearle

BeBee: https://www.bebee.com/bee/geoff-hudson-searle

Author of '*Meaningful Conversations*' https://meaningfulconversationsbook.com

Blog: www.freedomafterthesharks.com

CHAPTER 4

You Can Do Whatever It Is You Set Your Mind To

By Melissa Myers, CFP®

It's a sunny, spring day in 2018. The kind of day where the sun has warmed the room enough to warrant opening the windows and doors allowing cool, fresh air, inside. I sit in the sun watching the ducks play in the water. A pair of bald eagles are perched in a tree in front of me. Laughing to myself, I think, "*Who needs a TV? Mother Nature is the ultimate entertainment center.*"

Spring Lake has provided me with entertainment and inspiration over the years. I've had a lot of fun in the sun, boating with friends on the very lake I'm now lucky enough to live on. Twenty years ago, if you and I were boating on Spring Lake, and you told me, "*One day you're going to live up there, on that hill, in your brand-new house, with an in-ground pool, and you'll have paid cash for your last four vehicles,*" I wouldn't have believed you.

Over the last couple of decades I've kept in mind my mom's encouraging words: "*You can do whatever it is you set your mind to*." While I can't remember the events or circumstances of my childhood and teen years that led to conversations when my mom spoke these encouraging words, I've adopted and applied the belief, time and time again.

Perhaps my mom, read *Think and Grow Rich*, and was giving me her interpretation of what Napoleon Hill wrote and taught.

"Whatever your mind can conceive and believe,
your mind can achieve."

— Napoleon Hill

In first grade I took gymnastics. I loved the challenge, and I wasn't scared. There was one stunt that I really wanted to be able to do: "*The Penny Drop*." I hung by my knees, on the lower bar of the uneven parallel bars. I swung back and forth as I tried to get enough momentum so that I would be able to release my knees and land on my feet. Time after time, I fell. At some point, the coach looked at me and said, '*You might want to stop that so you don't get hurt*.' I wasn't dissuaded. Rather, I was determined. I knew I could do it; I just needed to keep trying. That very night, after many falls, I finally nailed the stunt. In my mind, I knew I could do a Penny Drop. I kept trying until I finally succeeded.

In high school, Mr. Pattison taught the typing class. Mr. Pattison, would have us cover our keyboards with a piece of paper and dictate the keys we were to type: "*f, d, s, a, space, j, k, l, sem*."

Driven to perfection, each night as part of my winding down process, I'd lie in bed and "*type*." "*I-h-a-v-e-a-b-i-o-l-o-g-y-t-e-s-t-t-o-m-o-r-r-o-w*." I don't know how I ever thought to visualize myself typing each letter of every word in my thoughts. What I do know is that the visualization exercise was highly effective; my speed and accuracy improved significantly by the end of the year.

After nearly 10 years of skiing, I got serious and took lessons. The instructor taught me to visualize the path my skis would take based on the instructions I gave my body. Use your feet to turn your skis. Your outside ski is the ski you put pressure on, in order to turn. When you want to turn left, put your weight on your right ski. When you want to turn right, shift your weight from your right foot to your left foot. You can ski any run here, if you stay in control. When you're on the chairlift, envision yourself making perfect turns, starting at the top and all the way down the entire hill. On the chairlift, in the car, and before I fell asleep each night, I would execute perfect runs in my mind. By the end of the season, my turns were fluid, and I was confident on the black diamonds.

In my thirties, my BHAG, Big Hairy Audacious Goal, was to pay off my mortgage before I turned forty. I believed I could and I did! How did I accomplish such a big goal?

First, I had to go into debt. Going into debt was easy. When I bought my first car, I got a loan. When I turned 18, I applied for a credit card, actually, many credit cards. College? Student loans. Clothes? Credit cards. Car maintenance? Credit cards. Vacations and restaurants? Credit cards.

When I was 26 and about to move for a new job I received advice from many well-intentioned people. Buy a house. Making mortgage payments is better than paying rent. You're building equity.

A short time after I bought my first house, I was hired at Morgan Stanley Dean Witter as a Financial Advisor. Two years later, I was struggling to hit my numbers. I didn't have marketing expertise or referral sources to help me bring in new clients and be successful. Each month, I was going deeper and deeper into debt. Amassing debt is easy. Getting out of debt is a challenge.

Eventually, I started to feel the stress of having too many bills and not enough income. The other thing I started to struggle with was shame and embarrassment. I'd been a financial advisor for two years, yet I was the one who needed advice. While I taught my clients how to invest and how to protect themselves with various forms of insurance, I was unable to help them with basic money management. I decided to quit my job as a financial advisor. Not long after I quit, I took a position as a licensed sales assistant in another Morgan Stanley office.

Budget Your Time and Money

Even though, I went from commission to salary when I took the sales assistant position, I continued to go deeper into dept. Scared into desperation, and humbled, in September 2003, I allowed my sister, Becky, to help me make a budget. She also lovingly told me to quit the gym, stop tanning, and stop getting my nails done. She gave me Dave Ramsey's book, Financial Peace, and I learned about Dave's famous debt snowball.

I began to budget my time and money. I began to act with intention. Exercising Personal Initiative, I humbled myself and followed my sister's advice. First a student, later a teacher, I planned ahead for expenses and created a get-out-of-debt plan.

I began saying, "*no*" to things that cost money and weren't adding value to my life. People thought I was cheap. Others wondered why I wrote checks to myself. Those checks were my "*allowance*" or spending money for the week. I budgeted my money over time.

Track. Project. Adjust. Repeat. It became apparent that I needed more income. I decided to become a Pampered Chef consultant. After all, I loved to cook. I thought, if I could cook and earn money while helping others get the right tools in their kitchens it was a bonus. Also, by working some extra nights and weekends, I wouldn't spend money I didn't have.

The decision to become a Pampered Chef consultant was one of the best decisions I ever made. Why? A guest at one of the "*parties*" decided to become a consultant. While I was training her to be a great Pampered Chef consultant, she recognized something in me that I didn't see in myself.

She knew I'd been a financial advisor, was currently a licensed assistant, and that Pampered Chef was my side-hustle. She said, "*You need to be advising, not assisting. Give me your resume*."

She worked at a bank and passed my resume on to a co-worker. The co-worker passed my resume on to his competitor at another bank. I got the job as a Financial Advisor/Associate Team Leader!

The week I started my new job, we had a corporate sales conference. At dinner one night, one of my peers told me, "*You just got the opportunity of a lifetime. This job can be life changing...if you do it right*." I'll never forget those words.

After about nine months into my new position and my learning curve, I still was struggling to meet my sales goals. I began to question whether I should even be a Financial Advisor.

One morning, while getting ready for work, I prayed, "*God, if you want me to be a Financial Advisor, please put the people in front of me that you want me to help.*"

By Applied Faith

Within a month, two very significant things happened. One, at the next sales conference, we were told to set a goal of selling $35,000 in investments per day. If we did that, we'd hit our goal. OK. Great! And thank you! Now I had a numeric goal to pursue.

The second thing that happened was, that my manager asked me if I would like to cover some other offices. This was THE opportunity I'd been waiting for. I was so excited. Armed with a numeric sales goal and the opportunity to work in offices that had the potential to produce higher numbers, I began to meet success, personally and professionally.

At that time, we were paid quarterly, based on the sales we had written. The last week of the quarter came with a big "*push*" from corporate to sell as much as possible. Driven to hit my sales goals, I pushed myself.

Up to that point I lived on a budget and paid a little bit each month toward my debt, but it was taking a long time. The "*end-of-quarter-push*" paid off. The incentive was large enough so that I was able to pay off $10,000 worth of debt! My quarterly incentive check was truly life changing.

The taste of financial reward fueled my drive and further motivated me. It also gave me confidence that I could earn enough to dig myself out of a deep hole of debt. Every incentive check went toward debt. Credit cards, student loans and a loan from my mother-in-law were paid off. After that, it was my car loan.

A short time later, my boss told me he was taking a position elsewhere and that I should let our regional manager know that I was interested in the Team Leader position.

The next day, the regional manager and I met. He didn't make any promises. Even without a promise, I acted in good faith that the job would be mine.

The Extra Mile

For three months, I fulfilled responsibilities of the role and acted as if I already had the promotion. I believed if I demonstrated my capabilities and went above and beyond that which was expected of me, I would get the promotion. What surprised me was my quarterly incentive check. While I hadn't been given the title, I received the compensation. Management paid me as if I was the Team Leader. Shortly after I received the largest check of my life, I received the official promotion!

Definiteness of Purpose

In a position where I was able to help clients and train others how to help clients, I found fulfillment and confirmation. I fully knew that I was doing what I was meant to do. God put opportunities in front of me, and

I embraced them. 'd found my opportunity to live my life with definiteness of purpose.

I learned from my personal struggles with money and used that experience to help friends, clients and colleagues make changes and improve their financial situations. While money is important, I understood that people matter more than money. I approached others with a servant mentality: *"How can I help you?"* "What are you working on?" *"What are your goals?"*

Establish a Mastermind Alliance

It takes a team to build success. Monday morning meetings were a time to brainstorm and collaborate, a time to share best practices. We knew that three minds were better than two, and without knowing what a mastermind alliance was, we acted as a mastermind. Rather than complain about change or challenges, we would ask questions. How can we get this done? What do we need to learn? What do we need to do? There's got to be a better way.

One idea led to another. We learned from each other. We trusted one another. We held each other to a higher standard. Achieving 100% wasn't good enough. We decided to set our goal at 130%, and we surpassed that too.

We maintained a **positive metal attitude** about success.

Budget Your Time and Money

Having budgeted my time and money paid off. I **went the extra mile** and studied for industry exams that weren't required of me. I earned licenses and the CERTIFIED FINANCIAL PLANNER™ designation. The more I studied, the less time I had to watch TV or spend money. The investment I made in myself led to more opportunities.

Over the course of six years and a divorce, I paid off all of my debt including my mortgage, while still being able to travel and have an in-ground pool installed. Most people will tell you that a pool is a waste of money. If you don't use it, I'd agree. However, some of my best memories are of time spent with friends and family in that pool. I feel I got every dollar's worth and more!

Cultivate Creative Vision

In 2010 I started to date Ryan. He liked to go out on his boat and I liked to go into my backyard and enjoy the pool. While dating I wondered how we could have both a pool and a boat without all the hassle of packing, loading, unloading and unpacking with every excursion. There might be a better way.

Poolside one evening, I suggested, "*If we had a house on the water with a pool, I'd go for a boat ride with you whenever you wanted*." We started to look at waterfront homes for sale on Zillow.

Property values were still quite low due to the Great Recession. We crunched some numbers and were ready for a new challenge. We decided we could buy a waterfront home. We just wouldn't live in it right away. For five summers we would rent the lake house as a weekly vacation rental. After five years, we would sell the house we lived in, use the proceeds to pay off the vacation rental, remodel it, and move to the water.

We made an offer on a lakefront home in September 2011. We closed on our waterfront home, and I sat for the CFP® exam in November. We got married in December.

I accomplished my goal of paying off the mortgage before I turned forty. I found out that I'd passed the CFP® exam in the spring of 2012. Life was going according to plan.

It was around that time that I started to get bored with my job. I began to feel a disconnect between how I wanted to serve my clients and the culture in which I worked. You need to have at least four sales appointments a day. What are you doing to make sure you hit your numbers? Melissa, what's going on with your offices? We're going to introduce your new comp plan for the upcoming year. It only has a few changes.

I began to feel a strange sense of anxiety. The interesting thing is that I wasn't anxious or overwhelmed with tasks and projects. Up to this point, most of my free hours were spent studying, designing a backyard, building out an unfinished basement, planning a wedding, and starting a vacation rental business.

I was anxious because I had nothing new and creative to do. I'd accomplished all my goals, I hadn't made any new goals, and I began to drift.

Learn from Adversity and Defeat

I didn't drift for long. Shortly after I received the letter congratulating me on having passed the CERTIFIED FINANCIAL PLANNER™ exam, I had a new goal. I applied for a regional manager position, which would entail managing Team Leaders. Armed with experience in leadership, I was ready for a new challenge and opportunity. I was confident in my ability to lead. Decision makers had other ideas as to where I would be most useful. Why take a successful producer out of production? I didn't get the management position.

In August 2012, I decided to leave corporate America and start an independent financial planning practice with my friend and colleague, Karmen.

Over the years we had disciplined ourselves to **budget our time and money**. That put us in the financial position to build our business from the ground up without incurring any debt. Over five years later, I have no regrets. I'm grateful that I didn't get that regional management position because it prompted me to set an even bigger goal.

Combine Personal Initiative with Definiteness of Purpose

It takes a lot of **personal initiative** to start and run a successful business. When faced with the challenges of running a business, I remind myself that I'm serving others as they seek to improve their position in life. It's my **definiteness of purpose**. It's what drives me to stay focused. I love to see others overcome adversity and achieve their goals and dreams.

In the financial world you can find success by doing high volume or you can be strategic with fewer, yet bigger clients. At the bank, we had a large team, and we did high volume. As an independent advisor, we had neither the volume or large team. Logic told me, "*It's time to find your niche*."

I ran client demographic reports and started to identify a few trends. However, the data didn't clearly suggest that I had any specific niche.

Actions Prove the Practicality of Our Imaginations

A few months into opening my financial planning practice, I partnered with Wendy Schweifler to give "Health and Wealth" presentations. Wendy asked Tony Rubleski to coach us. Soon after, Tony and Paul Guyon invited me to join their Mastermind group. I was introduced to *Think and Grow Rich, The 4-Hour Workweek*, and *CEO Space International*.

CEO Space International helped me get clarity about two challenges. One, while I wanted to "*niche down*" to fewer, bigger, better clients, I had a burning desire to help people who were without significant wealth. My heart was telling me to serve those who had financial challenges and were ready to take the steps toward improving their financial situation. My challenge was how to serve both a niche, with wealth, and people without wealth.

Imagination

CEO Space International staff helped me see that I could serve both groups at the same time. Many of the staff had clients with whom they worked with on an individual basis. They also had multiple income streams from sources which included physical books, e-books, courses they created and group coaching. They put on exclusive events, created membership groups and websites, wrote blogs, and did public speaking.

How did they do all of that? They created products they could sell and they built scalable businesses. A-ha! I could do that too! I could serve both my niche clientele along with the mass market by creating a scalable business model.

The second item of clarity was around my desire and ability to "*give back*" financially. One afternoon, Berny Dohrmann gave us the opportunity to make a public announcement. He asked us to stand up and share what it was that we committed to implement once we got back home. Having carried student loan debt into my 30's I decided to start a scholarship fund. My objective was to help reduce or eliminate the need for recipients to have student loan debt.

Back home, three months later, I met with Holly Johnson, from the Grand Haven Area Community Foundation, and on July 8, 2015, I'd signed the agreement where I committed to making monthly contributions to start a scholarship fund.

Enthusiasm and Concentration

That summer I read *The 4-Hour Workweek*. Next, I searched for blogs and podcasts on passive income.

Pat Flynn's, Smart Passive Income, came up in Google. Each morning I listened to his podcasts while I got ready for the day. I learned about passive income from affiliate marketing. Then an idea popped into my head. I would create a blog and the money I made from affiliate sales would help me get the scholarship fund fully funded ahead of schedule.

Thanks to Suzy Whitford at Start a Mom Blog, I learned how to build my sunkissedandblessed.com website, write blog posts, and make images for Facebook, Pinterest, Instagram and my blog posts. Through online courses, podcasts, and webinars I recognized a framework existed where I could create and deliver information online with courses, books, podcasts, blogs, classes, and video.

Applied Faith

"*OK, but how do I put it all together?*" I knew it could be done. I just didn't know how. My question was answered by my coach, Robyn Crane. Robyn taught me how to build programs and packages so that I can serve my clients at a higher level.

Had I not been willing to try new things, meet new people, or engage in generosity of time, money, and expertise, I wouldn't be serving the clients that I am today. Nor would I be able to serve the people whom I'll be serving in the future. Due to my personal initiative I've accomplished more than I ever thought possible. Because of applied faith I know that this is just the beginning and more great things are yet to come. As I achieve goals, I'll set bigger goals centered around my definiteness of purpose, helping people!

"Whatever your mind can conceive and believe, your mind can achieve."

A component of our original, five-year, vacation rental plan, was that we would do a major remodel of the lake house before we moved into it. The timeline changed, when we sold the house we lived in, two years early. We lived in the lake house for three years and didn't do any improvements because we knew we'd remodel soon. I wanted to remodel and use as much of the existing structure as possible to keep what we could out of a landfill.

Many people told us we'd be better off if we did a complete demo and started from scratch. In my naivety, I didn't believe them. Confident that a remodel was the way to go, we had our pool installed.

After nearly two years of research, planning, pinning to my Pinterest boards, and ongoing meetings with an architect, we were ready for bids from builders. The people who told us to tear down and start over were right. The bids came in excessively higher than planned and beyond what we wanted to spend, especially on a remodel. I was crushed, not to mention, mentally exhausted. I'd spent hours and hours and hours of my time researching and planning the remodel.

However, I'm not a quitter. I went back to the drawing board, literally. A year later, we have moved into our brand-new home. It cost substantially less than the remodel estimates, much closer to our original budget, and is laid out and designed to our taste and lifestyle. The pool is done, the boat will be coming out of storage soon and we're ready to enjoy summer in West Michigan!

Build A Positive Mental Attitude.

Despite challenges, set-backs and adversity I've been able to create plans and implement them to achieve goals. I remember my mom's words of encouragement and focus on getting an answer to my question, "*How am I going to…?*"

Today, I'm humbled and grateful. I've learned from my challenges and I use those experiences to serve others as they seek to improve their position in life---**My definite purpose!**

TRIBUTE TO TOM

"You can do it."

Tom,

I am grateful for you, your beliefs, and the work you did to make the world a better place. Although we never met in person, your emails and words of encouragement, "*You can do it*," motivate and inspire me to do work that makes this world a better place. Thank you for allowing me to contribute to Volume 9 of Journeys to Success.

Warmly,

Melissa Myers

Melissa Myers, CFP® | Bio

"God, if you want me to be a Financial Advisor, please put the people in front of me that you want me to help." Melissa Myers, CFP® had her prayers answered. She has been in the financial services industry since 2000. In 2012 she earned the CERTIFIED FINANCIAL PLANNER™ certification and co-founded Kar-Mel Financial Planners.

Melissa is an excellentist. She pours her love into everything she values. Faith, family, friends, hobbies and clients. Her approach to others, is with a servant mentality. *"How can I help you?" "What are you working on?" "What are your goals?"*

Myers believes in the power of community and values the importance of giving back. She is a member of All Shores Wesleyan Church, where she donates her time as a budget counselor in both, the Good $ense budgeting ministry and the Faith and Finances ministry.

Myers is a member of the Lake Michigan Estate Planning Council, Counterpart, the Grand Haven Eagles, and Tri-Cities Women Who Care. Additionally, she's established a scholarship fund through the Grand Haven Area Community Foundation.

A self-proclaimed foodie, Myers is always in search of fabulous restaurants specializing in unique and amazing cuisine. At home she loves cooking, boating, and relaxing poolside with a great book. She stays active by skiing, snowboarding, playing tennis, and going to spin class.

Myers thrives in Spring Lake, Michigan with her husband, Ryan and son, Brock.

To connect with Melissa, visit her at:

Kar-Mel Financial Planners, Sunkissed and Blessed

Karmelfp.com, sunkissedandblessed.com

melissa.myers@lpl.com, sunkissedandblessed@gmail.com

231-733-1166 & 231-206-0061

CHAPTER 5

On my Journey to Success: Clean Electricity Forever

By Dr. Alexandre Pavloski, P. Eng.

Instead of Introduction...and in memory of Tom Cunningham, The Success Coach

When we recall our lives we always think about people that were or are around us - sometimes with joy, sometimes with sadness, sometimes with questions. Less often – very rare – we think about the people that dramatically changed our path on the Journey to Success. They helped to make this path straightforward – but also to find necessary and timely turns. And – they made the Journey on this path AMAZING. This chapter is dedicated to the memory of these people – my mentors and business partners, my friends and family – and to the memory of Tom Cunningham, who saw a glimpse of "*amazing*" in everything we do on our journeys to happiness and success.

Part 1: Understanding Myself in a Sustainable Future

Starting point: childhood in St. Petersburg

I was born in mid 20th century in St. Petersburg. The city was built in very early seven-hundreds as a European capital of a great empire, and from these years evolved as a unique architectural ensemble, the Venice of the North. For those who visited St. Petersburg and had an opportunity to stay – walking this city was a great experience. For those who lived there, played in the parks of the city and touched its stones, it was an enjoyable practice. As a kid, I browsed the granite embankments of the Neva River, watching the facades of amazing palaces, and stepped onto their treasure galleries – weekly and daily. I fantasised about the architects of the past – and thought about the world of the future. The baroque and classical ensembles of the city enlightened these dreams, and hours and hours spent in the Hermitage helped me find a way in my life, a way I was ready to follow.

As I grew older, my visions moved this thinking through the city's theatres and concert halls. Philharmonia, St. Petersburg Philharmonic Society which opened its doors to many in late 19th century, allowed everybody to learn and enjoy. The Philharmonia has its unique music halls, and listening to the Orchestra performances of classical music from the balconies of its large hall informed my preferences. Progressing as a schoolboy, I also started my opera and ballet adventures in Mariinski Theatre spending my nights at the theatre's balconies to listen and watch.

When I spoke about museums and theatres of my childhood, that of course was not all. The beaches and pines of the Russian Westnorth - The Gulf of Finland which embraces the waters of the Neva river – gave me inspiration through annual months of summer vacations. That's where sports were mingled with mushroom hunting, and biking – with singing.

So – what in these beautiful days and nights of my childhood was related to my journey to success? What was my real problem, or was any problem there?

Well, indeed there was a problem. Being an economy and technology task of the humankind, it was not personal in my young life but I saw it as personal. The problem was simple: in mid-seventies the world understood energy crisis is critical, and the solution I saw for that was "clean electricity once and forever". Through many things learned in my physics classes at school, I felt this "clean electricity" mission was not clear to so many - as well as my role in it. I needed to explain this mission, to move and explore – this is where my life made a starting turn.

Student Studies in St. Petersburg, Polytechnic University

Choosing my university studies, I felt I was on my target. Many great ideas were discussed at those times, and in my "*clean electricity*" solution superconductivity and low plasma were at highest ranks. But – to play with these substances, you would be equipped with many methodologies and tools, and the industry did not have that skillset. This is why after some discussions and negotiations with the family and advisors I committed myself to theoretical studies on electricity for industrial applications. The Polytechnic University of Peter the Great in St. Petersburg positioned itself as a leader in multidisciplinary research, advanced technologies and innovations, and I dreamed to be a part of it.

My first years of education were committed to methods and studies for electrical circuits, and people around me knew how to do it well. By the end of second year after having trained my practical polytechnic skills I started being involved in the "*team of six*" – a small group that studied methods in electrical circuits and electromagnetic fields. Day after day we researched, tested and presented the ways to model and calculate these circuits and fields, and trained our knowledge. My studies started being focused on new technologies for magnetohydrodynamic power generation – an opportunity many researchers in the world put in the "*clean electricity*" basket. By early 1981 I completed the studies with my Master of Science in Applied Physics and joined a very advanced team in a state government institution.

Young Engineering Years

The name of the institution I started my engineering practice was called "*Direct Current Institute*" – the Research Institute for High-Voltage Direct Current Electric Power Transmission. It provided almost all Russian projects for transmissions with DC inserts, addressing high-voltage lines from 330 kV to 1150 kV, providing research, implementation, and overall project management.

From my first days I joined the team developing a 1 GW "back-to-back" HVDC substation in the town of Vyborg connecting Russia with the Scandinavian electricity network. As a young engineer, I participated in the commissioning of three units of this powerful 1GW station. With addition of the fourth one and related modernization in 2001, and a total transmission rating of 1.4 GW, the Vyborg substation was the world's largest HVDC-back-to-back facility until the 1.8 GW Al-Fadhili facility was completed in Saudi Arabia in 2009.

The opportunities of developing HVDC stations and connecting them to clean energy resources were attractive, and my mind started working in this clear direction. The institution already started developing solutions for a very unique at that moment magnetohydrodynamic (MHD) power plant in Russia, and my role gravitated to modeling and controls of MHD generators equipped with advanced inverters. My research work on this project evolved well; in 1986 I also completed my PhD on power conversion at the ITMO University in Saint Petersburg, one of Russia's National Research Universities.

While material advancements with low plasma canals and powerful magnets of MHD generators did not allow researchers to move this technology to large scale deployment, this did not stop my dreams of clean electricity. Power conversion moved me further and further and I got deeply involved in utility-scale wind and solar power generation. The scale of solar in the times of change in energy markets moved me also to better understanding the value of distributed energy resources.

Defining Sustainable Future

To understand the importance of clean energy resources, in 1991 I joined the team of professionals developing and testing environmental programs in the Central European University, an American university in Budapest, Hungary supported by George Soros. Selection of this rather unique team brought together a very small group of researchers and engineers from every Central European country. Being on the team, understanding the concepts of sustainable energy and finding future partnerships became a part of my life. While moving into these concepts, I understood the value of real time information management where Geographic Information Systems (GIS) were seen as a basic tool for clean electricity such as solar and wind. Very young but already available infrastructure using personal computers and cell phones started moving all this in a very practical direction.

Starting my First Business

After my work at CEU and related trips to Budapest the concept of "*clean electricity*" business started shaping my thoughts. However, it took me a year to complete my current projects and start my very first venture. I established my small headquarters in St. Petersburg and started my travels to the lands of small wind and solar.

The "*clean electricity*" world was growing, and there was a reason for its advancements, much more powerful in my mind than distributed energy resources themselves. This reason was called "a velvet revolution" in power conversion. Indeed, in 1980-ies power converters embedded in solar power plants had very small specific capacity (in terms of W per cubic meter). The "*velvet revolution*" in mid-nineties changed this situation by changing the semiconductor industry, producing higher capacity transistors at increasing speed, and boosting the specific capacity of converters one order of magnitude or more.

As a result in the industry, powerful converters for solar and wind power plants started moving on the market in early nineties. My focus on these advanced converters brought me in 1996 to Arlington, WA where an innovative team at Trace Engineering moved this business ahead. After some training at Arlington I started my international business activities with advanced converters for solar. Multiple market developments in the power converter business front such as acquisition of Trace Engineering Corporation by Xantrex in 2000 and related spin-off of OutBack Power, made me better realize the coming mainstream changes in the industry. And – my thinking about information technologies that would drive the inevitable future of "*clean electricity*", the thinking that had grown on the seeds of sustainable development work initiated in 1991, started shaping better the next step in my life.

Mastering Skill in Innovation

To move me to the next level, it was not enough to succeed in my engineering consultancy and related business; it was important to review and revise my skill in managing innovation in clean energy management. And a great opportunity evolved: my "alma mater", the State Polytechnic University and Penn State University started an MBA program in innovation management. This made a great timing for my business planning. In 1999-2000 I completed an advanced executive program that included key innovation management ingredients in micro- and macroeconomy, information technologies in innovation, statistics as a base for artificial intelligence, and advances in operational and financial management. The program included many important aspects related to "*clean electricity*" such as social management and psychology, leadership, decision-making, quality management and human resources. The program went well, and I was very excited. My readiness to move had taken one more turn.

Starting My Journey to Success

When I started preparing myself to my path in innovation management, it was necessary to define the best starting point for my business journey – geographically, clean electricity-wise and professionally. It was also important to select a starting point rich of business and family friendships, and my family supported this approach.

I knew that since the beginning of 90ies Germany started leading in clean electricity deployment. One leadership area was related to hardware manufacturing and installation of solar photovoltaic (PV) panels and windmills. Another area was related to electricity policy instruments: Germany started rapidly transitioning to clean electricity through feed-in tariffs - a guaranteed price established for anyone who wanted to sell clean electricity to the grid, and a guarantee that they would have access to the grid to do so.

I felt that missing in the key portfolio for clean electricity deployment was data and information critically needed for planning, deployment and operations of clean electricity plants - as well as for transmission, distribution and consumption of this electricity. Energy management was a pillar of clean electricity on the market, and information technologies to support this pillar had to be in place. This was my target, and the centres of energy-related IT development and innovation were in North America.

There was a close connection between IT and clean energy resources in North America; I had to find this connection, and it waited for me. From my experience with HVDC power plants and related electricity resources I knew well the work in Canada. From my research I also knew that Atlantic Canada, and specifically the province of Nova Scotia has an amazing potential to become a Saudi Arabia of the West – not for oil but for clean electricity. Indeed, the core electricity resources were there: unique tidal (up to 18 m of tidal in the Bay of Fundy), very strong wind (with capacity factors exceeding 40%), great solar resources for urban use (higher than in Germany) and potential connections with large-scale hydro resources in Newfoundland and Labrador. The history later showed my expectation as Emera, a leading energy group in North America, and its partners started building a HVDC loop in Atlantic Canada. This addressed limitations to wind and tidal deployment, and operational access of clean electricity sources to their clients in North America. A choice for 100% clean electricity society in Nova Scotia was my personal urban choice, and my decision was made. In 2003 my new company – Green Power Labs – started its operations with headquarters in Halifax, Nova Scotia.

Part 2: On my Clean Electricity Path

Three Steps to the Future

Green Power Labs started its activities as a team of three founders. Its long-term business plan included the three key steps:

- Consulting provincially, nationally and internationally: matching our value proposition and service to that of the market; that allowed us to adjust our strategic thinking
- IT/OT Technology Development: moving our technology of predictive analytics to the development of predictive controls where predictive analytics is the key input
- Demonstration and Commercialization: proving the value and increasing sales in the markets where clean electricity is of high value

Predictive Energy Management: To the Product of Tomorrow

We knew that the value of energy was already well understood in 18th and 19th century. It has been critically re-visited during the 1970ies energy crisis, a period when the major industrial countries of the world faced substantial petroleum shortages and elevated prices. This crisis started a global effort to bring clean electricity in and make it replace fossil fuels, which have clear limits, and long-term product needs. The focus on renewable energy had been determined, and technologies and products started being developed. The scale of clean electricity started growing by early 2000-s, moving the market and defining the limits and implications related to access to this electricity in the current grids. A critical next step in removing these limits had a name: Predictive Energy Management (PEM).

Green Power Labs had a vision for clean electricity chain where PEM would be a chief "*dispatcher*". This chain started with clean electricity generation plants like solar or wind plants, proceeded with utilities' transmission and distribution grids and ended at electricity consumption in commercial buildings and residential houses. PEM for this chain seemed to us an efficient "*agent*", and it had its "*clients*": Smart Power Plants, Smart Grids, Smart Buildings and Smart Cities. In the thinking of market and industry leaders, the Smart Energy concept was growing, and PEM was in the core of it. And - it had two steps: Predictive Analytics (Information Technology - from planning to operations) and Predictive Controls (Operational Technology - in operations only).

Predictive power analytics encompassed a variety of advanced techniques that analyze current and historical facts to predict future events in power generation, transmission and distribution, and effectively prepared for impending impacts. With the rapid changes in how electrical power is generated and distributed, the business case for integrating and utilizing predictive power analytics in clean electricity chain had become very compelling.

Predictive power controls applied as an automated operational technology leveraged the value of real time predictive data leading to significant savings in clean electricity operations. It streamlined interconnection of PV power plants with hosting power grids, and enabled PV power plants to support operating conditions in the grid thus facilitating the smooth deployment of PV power worldwide.

The growing share of solar power and other clean electricity sources, both at utility-scale and distributed generation levels, had made predictive power analytics and predictive controls services and applications critically important for all key clean electricity operations and my team focused its effort to unleashing clean electricity in existing power grids.

Indeed, "*unleashing*" clean electricity meant "*solar roofs everywhere*" – and definitely in North America. Many things already happened that moved the world to this "*destination*": reduction in solar costs to below 50 cents per watt, change in energy policies such as Feed-in Tariff (FIT) due to rapid growth of residential solar in some jurisdictions, changes in the market moving utilities to delivering electricity from their clients' roofs. Yes, it meant generating clean electricity and using it at every house. But it also meant much more – the growth of electric vehicles and home batteries, which moved the chain from one-way to two-way (bi-directional) power flow. We saw the rise of residential battery storage becoming a new reality; we also saw technical upgrades and highest growth in lithium ion batteries for residential storage. That allowed for bringing the backup power solutions of yesterday to some new heights. All this needed to be addressed – and addressed promptly.

Predictive Analytics: An Inevitable Phase

With Predictive Analytics, we clearly saw the opportunities and challenges of creating a smart energy future. We also understood a secure, resilient, diversified energy future demands integrated, adept and robust predictive models that work in real time. That's why we started developing a strong multidisciplinary team that had promptly built a reputation for exceptional quality of knowledge base and service. This magical interplay between science and know-how had resulted in immediate positive response from our clients.

Based on this success, we started working on innovative, leading-edge technologies and solutions for predictive analytics that allowed our clients to manage risk and optimize effectiveness of energy management. Green Power Labs addressed three major time horizons: strategic planning (up to 25 years); deployment (1 to 5 years) and operations (next minute-next hour-next day). To address these horizons, we developed unique satellite imagery processing technology to monitor and forecast weather and energy at high spatial and temporal resolution. Its method was based on a physical model that relates the satellite-derived earth-atmospheric reflectivity from the visible channel of the satellites to the transmissivity of the atmosphere.

By completing in 2009 our proprietary technology platform, SolarSatData™, we made a good step in clean electricity movement - we covered distributed/rooftop and centralized/utility-scale solar power generation, transmission and distribution applications. We offered a comprehensive suite of predictive analytics services for solar power management embracing the complete life cycle of any solar power project.

Based on SolarSatData™ - Green Power Labs' advanced predictive technology platform, our services supported each major stage of a solar power project development: project site selection and feasibility rating, project deployment, and project operations. This included high resolution solar resource mapping and decision support for candidate sites selection, solar resource assessment at the candidate sites for the project bankability, virtual solar resource and power generation monitoring, and operational solar resource and power generation forecasting.

To support the decisions of our clients Green Power Labs utilized an advanced GIS-based decision support system that supports selection of candidate sites for solar power projects based on comprehensive high resolution solar resource data, land use and availability data, vicinity to power substations, road and railroad infrastructure, environmental considerations and other relevant spatial information.

The key component of the decision support system developed by Green Power Labs was its satellite-based high-resolution solar resource map. SolarSatData™ solar resource mapping technology was applicable to satellite data for any specific region of coverage, regardless of location and satellite data source. Based on the data sets produced, high spatial resolution solar resource maps were developed in a standard GIS format compatible with client practices.

Green Power Labs conducted comprehensive site-specific solar resource assessment utilizing its in-house satellite imagery processing technologies. Green Power Labs' SolarSatDataTM predictive platform produced hourly global horizontal and direct normal irradiance data sets for up to a 15-year period, conditional on the availability of satellite imagery archives.

Meanwhile, our SolarSatData™ – based virtual pyranometers monitored site-specific solar radiation conditions globally at best temporal and spatial resolution available from civil satellites. Combined with Green Power Labs' advanced solar power generation models, this virtual solar generation monitoring service provided support for solar power plant performance monitoring and maintenance. It also provided increased visibility of all distributed solar generation within utility service territory.

But – the key effort on and benefit from Predictive Analytics was related to operational solar power generation forecasting. Green Power Labs' solar forecasting technology was based on the physical relationship between cloud cover and solar radiation, utilizing best available, high-resolution numerical cloud cover forecasts from a combination of ensemble Numeric Weather Prediction models and satellite-derived information. This advanced proprietary technology enabled automated delivery of solar radiation and power generation forecasts for Day Ahead, Hour Ahead, and intra-hour forecasts at up to 5-minute granularity. Green Power Labs correlated solar radiation forecasts with ground observations and provided critical operational information.

Predictive Controls: The Key in Operations

While our results in Predictive Analytics on the clean electricity path made us very excited, our next destination started already forming in our minds. We knew that our analytical work required integration in real time operational realities to reduce or eliminate the limitations of generation, transmission/distribution associated with the consumption of clean electricity. The key to these operational realities was Predictive Controls. This new level of controls required high resolution input of weather and energy moved in artificial intelligence-based models and control optimization, and the team was capable of delivering the results needed.

EntroPBC: the new type of Building Control

In early 2012 Green Power Labs started its technology development of predictive controls for electricity consumption management in buildings.

Commercial and residential buildings consume about one-third of the world's total energy. Building heating and cooling is the single largest item in building energy consumption. It is also the most expensive item in building energy cost as power for heating/cooling is purchased at peak rates.

Predictive building control improves the efficiency of buildings energy use by anticipating and reacting to the changing weather conditions and requirements for heating and cooling in real time. Because weather and heating/cooling loads can vary significantly throughout the day, the impact of intelligent prediction is significant. EntroPBC enables predictive analytics services to provide critical weather and energy data for predictive building controls operations in real time, using this data to optimize building performance and minimize energy use, cost and carbon footprint.

Predictive Building Control is a supervisory control technology. It continuously (at 15 minute intervals) produces optimal control set points for building heating, ventilation and air conditioning (HVAC) operations and sends these set points to the Building Energy Management system (BEMS). This improves the HVAC system performance and minimizes building energy use, costs and carbon footprint while achieving better comfort conditions in buildings.

The value proposition that ignited our thinking was simple: to reduce building's energy costs and carbon footprint while increasing its thermal comfort.

EntroPBC unique features are:

- Operational weather and solar irradiation forecasting at building site and building walls, all in real time

- Solar irradiation forecasts for building roof and walls, all obstructions to sunlight considered, on clear-sky and cloudy days
- Artificial intelligence-based energy models forecast building energy use in real time
- Continuous learning sharpens PBC's control of the buildings' response to weather conditions
- As smart building brain, PBC develops multiple building energy use scenarios based on real time conditions and selects the option maximizing thermal comfort and minimizing energy use

The major benefits that drove our product development work were also simple for the people we were ready to serve: happier building owners (HVAC energy cost are reduced), happier tenants (Improved comfort in individual thermal zones), effective corporate sustainability leaders (reduced carbon emissions), more productive building managers (live building energy performance analytics), successful business development professionals (buildings better suited for today's more demanding and "green" focused tenants), and a great story for the President to share with the shareholders' annual meeting - a clear example of commitment to minimizing carbon footprint.

It took four years to bring the team to its first complete results in 2016, but these results were obvious – and amazing. We selected a LEED® Gold university campus building of 100,000 sq. ft floor area with its construction completed in September 2010. The work of our technology in the building in four months (from August to November 2016) reduced heating, ventilation and air conditioning costs by over 40%, and in October 2016 – 50%. And – following thermal comfort improvement, the building zones remained within the established indoor temperature range 92 percent of the time, up from 85 percent before. This was a success. To double- and triple-check our measurement and verification work, we brought technical auditors – and were treated by that: in October 2017 we were awarded by Efficiency Nova Scotia with its Bright Business Innovation Award.

And – this was a great entry to our successful commercialization of EntroPBC.

From Buildings to Microgrids....

To advance its skill and focus in predictive energy management, in parallel with our work on predictive controls for buildings in 2013 we started our work on predictive control for microgrids. The situation was very simple. We knew that energy intermittency in power feeders with high penetration of rooftop solar affects electricity frequency and voltage and, consequently, the grid stability. Existing grid assets in the distribution grid (e.g. on-load tap changers) are not designed for frequent response caused by energy intermittency which leads to their excess wear and related grid failures. To improve the reliability of operations in the grid, every PV plant has to first, support operating conditions at its connection to the grid (say, service transformer at a feeder), and only (but importantly!) second – to produce as much clean electricity as needed on the market. This capacity of distributed PV plants to participate in grid operations and fully support operating conditions like voltage and frequency in real time was not available for distribution grids until early 2010s when requirements to be equipped with smart inverter technology became a must. This was very important for utility-scale PV power plants to integrate predictive control techniques to enable compliance with and support of operating conditions in the grid. That was as well important for microgrids with distributed solar PV to remove any limitations related to installed PV capacity and energy intermittency.

As in other areas of our work with predictive control, we approached this problem from supervisory standpoint. Predictive Grid Control technology proposed by Green Power Labs was a supervisory control technology. It allowed for management of voltage and frequency, active and reactive power in the grid at any point of PV interconnection in real time. It also limited and addressed any challenges related to microgrid without any impact to a hosting grid. The technology presented an advanced solution for PV power plants allowing for easily meeting grid interconnection requirements. It also limited the impact of energy intermittency in the grid, supported the increased penetration of PV plants, and improved the performance of existing grid assets.

The major differentiator of Green Power Labs' predictive control technology for microgrids was its ability to provide supervisory control to multiple PV plants to support operating conditions in any circuit of the grid based on the predictive data generated by SolarSatData™ predictive platform. This enabled seamless integration of PV power plants in the grid at any level of PV penetration.

...and from Virtual Plants to MicroMarkets!

Thinking about predictive energy management for microgrids we focused our work and attention on predictive controls and many technical components of it. It was later in our thinking when we understood the following: clean electricity trade solutions are critically important for one simple reason - in the future with clean electricity everybody will be a prosumer, a person who consumes and produces clean electricity.

To address this future need, we started developing solutions for microgrids where the participants – "*prosumers*" – buy or sell clean electricity.

We began with net energy metering allowing consumers who generate some or all of their own electric power use to sell excess electric power into the distribution grid at times when it is not needed and consume electric power from the grid when required. This was particularly important with electric power generated by wind and solar energy. Electric power exchange with the grid in net metering arrangements is executed at the same retail price defined by the utility service provider, and consumers pay or are billed only for the difference between the electric power generated and consumed over a billing period. Thus, in net metering arrangements, the distribution grid provides consumers with a form of free electricity storage service while consumers provide the grid with electric power generating resources to meet power demands.

However, with the growing penetration of clean electricity resources in the distribution grid, the operating costs of maintaining standard operating conditions in the grid, such as voltage and frequency, may exceed the benefits of having access to electric power resources from consumers. This experience has resulted in the cancelling of net metering arrangements by a number of utilities and an evolving trend to limit or remove these arrangements from electricity retail practice. Such developments have been referred to as the "*end of net metering*".

This limitation and/or cancellation of net metering arrangements has created a new market situation in distribution grids and their segments equipped with advanced energy management tools. These tools enable consumers with power generation capacity to sell the excess generated power to other consumers/market participants within their grid segment or into other grid segments of the distribution grid. These activities have created new energy market opportunities for electric power exchange and sale, and we proceeded with our work on addressing these opportunities.

We also knew the retail market provides a "*gate*" for microgrid electric power and service trading to external markets. It was assumed that all microgrid prosumers having a contract with the microgrid operator ("MO") and trust that the MO will represent all of the MO's customers towards the external markets and will distribute the internal resources to the MO's customers in the best way respecting internal energy generation and consumption. We developed solutions for the MO to represent the microgrid as a Virtual Plant, have the MO sell/buy energy on the external market, and sell balancing and ancillary services.

However, we were aware of several problems with the operation of existing microgrids. One important problem with existing microgrid electricity trading platforms and existing electricity markets was the absence of solutions for real-time market management in microgrids with prosumers. In simple terms, at every moment prosumers were interested in selling to/buying from other prosumers in the microgrid in real time, and after that – in having the MO selling to/buying from an external grid.

A need therefore existed for solutions for real-time market management for microgrids with prosumers equipped with clean electricity resources. This concept included a technology and microgrid market management system for such a microgrid. While not yet requested by the market, these solutions were seen as a mainstream of the neighbouring tomorrow, and one of most practical ones. These are the solutions my team is working on now – on its Journey to Success with Clean Electricity Forever.

In Conclusion

This story, as others, are about the Journey to human success. Each of us in our lives experiences this Journey in many ways. We are happy when after many days and years of effort we achieve our destinations and celebrate with friends the triumphs and amazing successes. This Journey means our inevitable progress, and sharing with you some enjoyable moments, I was thinking about the pleasure of this unstoppable nature. It has been discovered before - and will be discovered much more.

DR. Alexandre Pavloski, P. Eng. | Bio

Dr. Pavlovski is an innovation leader, entrepreneur and professional engineer with over 35 years of expertise in clean energy. He holds a Master of Science, Applied Physics, and a Ph.D., Power Conversion degree, and diplomas and certificates in Environmental Policy and Innovations Management. His professional career has taken him through several increasingly challenging innovation management and entrepreneurship positions. Today, Dr. Pavlovski serves as President and CEO of Green Power Labs Inc.

Dr. Pavlovski is a member of Global Affairs Canada' Clean Technology Advisory Group. He has been representing Canada on several International Energy Agency's Tasks.

Dr. Pavlovski is a former chair of the Energy Advisory Council of the Halifax Chamber of Commerce and a Board Member of the Canada Green Building Council – Atlantic Chapter; he is a senior member of the Association of Energy Engineers, and a charter member of its Alternative & Renewable Energy Development Institute.

CHAPTER 6

From Becoming to Being

By Latha Sukumar

Background

As I sit here in Markham, Ontario, gazing out into our beautiful backyard, drenched in the sun on a warm spring day, I think back to where I was exactly 45 years ago. I was at my older sister's wedding, a 11 year old running around in a silk skirt, precocious and talkative, hanging out with all the adults, trying hard to be someone. I was in grade 6, living with my parents and siblings in a lush corner of Kerala, India. At school I got by doing as little as possible. My teachers said I was very bright but did not try hard enough. I was more into extracurricular activities and passionate about fighting against inequality. My mother tells me that at the age of 3, I rolled up one of two pretty dresses I had and gave it to our maid's daughter.

I also loved to be noticed and so took every opportunity to perform. I was selected for a radio show at the age of six. I loved elocution, debates and plays. I created and performed a mono-act of the entire Cinderella story and was Oliver in Oliver Twist. At age 12, I was crowned the school's best orator. At home I loved to debate adults on gender inequality and caste or class based discrimination. My parents were proud I had imbibed their values but reminded me that most people found girls who argued obnoxious. When I was in Grade 8, things changed. My father got transferred to Chennai, India. Not only did I leave friends, move to strange city in the middle of the school year, I had left behind my "*brand*". No one knew me here and so I was starting over. For the first time I was in a co-ed school. However, it was taboo in our conservative middle class social circles to be seen fraternizing with the opposite gender. But forbidden fruit is sweet, so when a couple of boys wrote me secret notes I was flattered and thrilled but also scared and conflicted. This new school was less about academics and all about sports. I felt completely inadequate, and obsessed over my humiliation at failing so badly at all activities requiring coordination. This was a painful blow to my fragile and developing ego. Also, I felt stifled and unable to freely express myself. It felt like my process of "*becoming*" someone was stunted. Two years later we moved to Mumbai where I completed grades 11 and 12. I was restless and unmotivated, so I squandered my chances of getting into a professional program. Also, no one at home was terribly concerned about my lack of commitment to securing very high grades. My father was keen to get me married. My mother was too exhausted and weighed down with housework to argue with him. They both came through for me in a big way later on and I will speak to that in a moment. I also want to say something about my mother since she has played a key role in what I was to become.

My mother cried when I was born because she did not want me to suffer the same fate as her. As a girl growing up in a patriarchal Brahmin household, near the temple city of Tanjore in South India, she had led a sequestered life, until her marriage. She could not attend school after puberty. She was determined her 3 daughters would not suffer her fate. We were raised listening to stories that had a feminist theme and were about oppressed women's subversive acts. Every story had a moral about some ordinary woman who showed courage and forbearance to triumph in the end. She reduced us to tears and roused our passion to take arms in solidarity with women-kind. No story was too adult for us. I knew about sexual molestation of widows in joint families and the taboo topic of marital rape early in my teens. So I owe to my mother the passion I have to work with our most vulnerable.

I graduated grade 12 with good grades but meandered aimlessly towards a Bachelor's degree in Sociology and English Literature. I was now in a women's college with snooty upper class kids who talked about a life I knew nothing about. I was embarrassed that we were poor in comparison, and so pretty much kept to myself. I was just not motivated to nurture my interests in social activism or my talents, debating and performing. I had bad allergies and my parents urged me to join a yoga therapy course, which I attended every day, after class. Who knew then that this would be the beginning of my life-long pursuit of yoga?!

I met my husband in the third and final year of my undergraduate program. My parents wanted to see me married and he was an eligible bachelor. There was a lot of emotional blackmail involved and I resigned myself to my fate. Also, what were the odds I would ever fall in love and marry, given how limited and controlled my interactions with boys were? I was married a month after my graduation and soon after left for Malaysia, where he worked.

I was just 21 and Malaysia, though a tropical paradise, was far away from home. I was homesick, lonely and frustrated because I was housebound. I became a good homemaker, since I had little else to do in our tiny village. However, since my culinary skills were the extent of my competence, I knew I was regressing. I was anxious to find a way out of my life of domesticity – become someone. I soon had a baby. The opportunity to move to Canada came in 1987. But the 25 year old who boarded that plane with an 18-month-old baby was very different from the young and carefree girl who had gotten married a few years earlier. I was in the throes of anxiety and depression, which I had developed, post-partum. The acute sense of my mortality I had experienced since childhood had compounded. I had low self-esteem and felt a loss of control over my destiny, much like a raft over the high seas. I was just living up to society's expectations of me. The birth of my child signaled additional responsibilities and sent me into a tizzy of debilitating anxiety attacks and post- partum depression. How was I going to elevate myself from obscurity and be noticed?!

In many ways my nervous breakdown had a positive outcome in that it forced me to overcome and look for purpose. It motivated me to take on my demons, become someone with power and influence - a lawyer and social entrepreneur.

Becoming

My first act of foolish courage was to resist being medicated. I used the advice of philosophers instead. In his book "*Why Fear*" the Indian philosopher J. Krishnamurthy had written, "*the thought is not the thing described*". That simple, yet profound mantra held the key to my transformation. I began practising mindfulness, without calling it that! Realising that fear is an emotion, brought on by my thoughts and not by anything external to me, was profound and life altering. Intellectually I knew I could not be spooked, belittled or mocked by them anymore. Of course, practising was by no means easy. Every time I allowed thoughts to rise unchecked, the anxiety and associated pain that they brought on, engulfed me. The temptation was to shut out the painful thoughts and escape into some pleasant daydream. But I resisted and faced them dispassionately. Gradually and magically my mind began to quieten. My negativity and limited worldview began to wear off and I saw boundless potential to grow. I just had the clarity to see life as it was, without the limiting veil of my conditioning.

So armed with my mindfulness practice, I boarded that plane to Canada a wide-eyed new immigrant with a little child. Even though my English was good, I was shocked to find out that I did not enunciate words with the right emphasis and tone to come across confident. I realized also that I needed to build my lexicon of stock phrases, "*how's it going*", "*way to go*", "*what's up*", learn to make small talk and to speak with conviction. The right look mattered and this meant mutating into a foreign being who dressed with studied casualness, shorn of the "ethnic" look. The process of remaking my identity was overwhelming. It took me a long time to become comfortable in my newfound persona and to speak up in public with conviction. It took even longer for people to sit up and take me seriously.

I got my first job, in telemarketing, 2 days after I landed. I learnt the art of the sale and immersed myself in improving my communication skills. In six months I was promoted to Supervisor. This boosted my confidence. However, I knew that I needed to do meaningful work that challenged me. I was obsessed with women's rights and wrote a paper on the feminist movement to include with my application to the Master's program in Women's Studies at York University. To my astonishment, I was accepted. I found myself coming into my own, finding my voice in a program, which hailed the "*personal to be political*". I found writing in the active voice extremely liberating. I wrote my research review paper on dowry related domestic violence in the South Asian community. I had an A average and could have gone on to do a PhD. However, I thought my activist heart would thrive in law. So my next stop was law school. I did my LSAT and applied to law schools in Toronto. My parents were visiting me in Canada when the acceptance came from Osgoode Hall Law School. Everyone decried my decision, saying law was not a profession for an immigrant woman. Except my parents and husband, who offered me unconditional support. It was a big decision especially because my husband found a job in another town and had to move. My daughter was with me and I had to balance an intense program with caring for her. I found myself a little out of my depth at first, not being familiar with the history or politics of Canada, but was among the top 25% in my first semester and among few to land a summer job at the Crown's office. Here I helped Crowns prosecute domestic violence and sexual abuse cases, and realised for the first time the barriers to justice that victims who spoke no English faced. I could understand their lack of faith in the system and their reluctance to testify against the men who abused them, usually their only family in Canada. I wanted to help but did not know how.

I graduated law school and articled with the Ministry of the Attorney General. Then Premier of Ontario Mike Harris, introduced a hiring freeze in government. I decided to hang up my shingle and become a community lawyer. An opportunity came to work as Executive Director of a small non-profit that helped victims of domestic violence. However, that day in September 1996, when I started my job at MCIS Language Solutions (Multilingual Community Interpreter Services (On)), as it was known then, in a tiny shop front in a grittty part of town, I had no idea I would end up where I am. I knew I liked what the agency did that's all. I knew I had to get through the month to rescue the agency from premature closure because government funding was about to be cut due to a lack of demonstrated need for the service. Thus began my journey at MCIS in a rough neighbourhood in Scarborough, Ontario, with just 1.5 other Full Time Equivalent (FTE), 40 interpreters and $150,000 budget. We had a service that could help women who were in situations of abuse; communicate in their own language. It seemed serendipitous that my cause had found me.

However, I was not without self -doubt. After a Masters and 4 years towards a legal education, all I had was a part-time law practice and role as an ED in an obscure agency that no one had heard about! Feelings of anxiety and questions around my place in life surfaced from time to time. On the other hand, I felt a deep sense of urgency to bring about meaningful change in the lives of women and children. Then one day I read in the papers about an Ontario Court Judge who had broken down on reading a Victim Impact

Statement. I found out that our interpreter had facilitated the victim's telling of her story through several arduous months of evidence gathering so the case could be successfully prosecuted. I heard similar stories every day. My conviction in MCIS's work and role grew more by the day.

On days when things did not go so well, I drew upon the wisdom of my late grandfather, who had said, no matter what you do, you show up for work every day. I decided to structure my life around certain routines that I abided by no matter what, and kept plodding on. I began a regular yoga practice every morning from 6 -7 at a local community centre and went to work from there. On several cold winter mornings there were just two of us. My practice helped me get in touch with my body. As I focussed on my breath and movement, my agitated mind simmered down and I was calm and clear. My practice anchored me to focus on what I had to get done each day and enabled me to set short term, achievable goals. The first challenge was to keep the lights on and get through the funding year. The second one was to scale up my operations so we could break free from our dependency on year-to-year government funding.

During my first 8 years at MCIS, we made small gains. Our annual grants grew so we could serve more people but they were restrictive leaving little room for maneuverability. MCIS' Board encouraged me to start a fee for service program. However, we had to first build capacity to deliver large volumes. So we secured short time project grants to do this. We got one to build a database to manage interpreter scheduling, invoicing and reports and others to run pilot projects as the one with the City to provide interpretation services for residents in refugee shelters. We also started a fee based interpreter-training program. These projects helped us diversify our funding sources, build capacity and contacts but the momentum to build a social enterprise was still not where we wanted it to be. We were still wholly dependent on government funding.

In early 2000s, we introduced our fee-based training for bilinguals to become interpreters. This ended up being a "*win-win*" for both MCIS and the trainees. We were looking for interpreters who would populate our database and would be available for "*on-call*" work and the thousands of professional newcomers entering Canada were looking for their first job opportunity, "*Canadian*" experience and a network of contacts. Our entry into training was our biggest coup. Today we are the largest trainer of language professionals in Canada, through in person and on-line programs. This approach held us in good stead in 2015 when the Canadian government put out a bid for an interpretation services contract on a one-week turnaround, to welcome 25,000 Syrian refugees into Ontario and Quebec. We had several hundred Arabic professional interpreters and bilinguals in our pipeline that we could immediately deploy!

Transitioning to Being

In 2004, my healthy and much beloved father was suddenly diagnosed with terminal cancer in India. I dropped everything and went on a leave of absence for 4 months till he passed, also staying back to support my mother and settle his affairs. I came back to a mess. MCIS staff was fighting with each other and funders were threatening to cancel contracts. I was only able to restore sanity to my personal and professional life because of a life changing experience I had in the summer of 2004, just before my father was diagnosed.

That experience was my first Vipassana course. Ten days of silence and meditation at a beautiful and serene retreat centre in the Laurentians. Here I had many epiphanies and began a transformation that has helped me gain in compassion and strength, to lead and grow a thriving social enterprise that serves several thousand vulnerable persons, victims of all forms of violence, homeless persons and individuals seeking access to critical information and services, besides providing employment opportunities to several thousand more. I did not realise it then, but my transition from "*becoming*" to "*being*" was set in motion with this course.

I began the slow process of breaking free from negative habit patterns. I realised that all my actions and reactions were tied to my conditioning. I craved good sensations and tried to perpetuate them and avoided behaviour that brought on painful ones. This affected how I interacted with the world and how people communicated with me. However, when I started to observe my sensations pleasurable or painful, with equanimity, and noticed associated reactions then I began to liberate myself from conditioned patterns of behaviour. Simply put, if someone said something to trigger a painful sensation, I became mindful of the behaviour that was set in motion, which I could now control, and change. I no longer looked outside me for excuses to justify my actions. I became more accessible because I was now in control of my reactions and therefore able to listen and respond with an open mind and heart.

I also became less resistant to change. In silent meditation we observe the rapidity with which thoughts and sensations change, and experience the futility of holding on to ephemeral matter, thoughts and ideas. By extension, when we embrace change then the opportunities in all situations appear boundless. Where previously a key staff's resignation would have brought on great anxiety, I was now able to recover quickly and look for the opportunities in this adverse occurrence.

However, the most profound realisation was this. All through life I had put in the effort to become something. I had constructed an image in my mind of who I was to myself and to the rest of the world. I was so identified with it that I had to preserve it at all costs and so my actions in the world aimed to serve this end. Now I realised I had to grow to be less not more. So when I began noticing self-serving actions, which helped me build and maintain that image, I stopped myself and tried instead to be authentic. This meant I was able to easily admit my mistakes, give up positions and not impose my views on others. I became less critical and more curious, less judgemental and more open and more of a listener than a talker. This shift was tremendous for the place it gave others to be their true selves with me.

MCIS benefited because I was no longer clinging to an image or position to define who I was. I was open to bringing in very smart people on my board and staff without feeling threatened, fully acknowledging to myself and others my weaknesses. So even though our problems loomed large in 2004, I was not overwhelmed. I approached all situations with some creativity and huge leaps of faith, looking to advisors and experts for support and guidance.

In 2006, we reached a low point. Our time limited funded projects had come to an end and our efforts to win fee for service contracts had no success. We were an agency waiting to happen. Six months into the fiscal year we had a big deficit. But we did not crumble under the stress. We stayed hopeful and focussed on the day to day. At this time we had a partnership with the Rotman School of Business which sponsored summer MBA interns to work with community based agencies and our intern helped us identify ways in which we could scale up operations should an opportunity come our way. He helped identify Call Centre solutions and system upgrade options. Here I must mention that effort born out of anxiety is counter-productive and leads to poor decisions. It's much better to relax into the space where you are and trust that things will happen if you just keep moving in the right direction, which is what we did. When I have done that, events have occurred and people appeared that I could not have imagined or fashioned with my mind. One such event occurred in September 2006. I received an unexpected phone call from a friend, who forwarded me a Request for Proposals to bid on. We bid not stopping to think if we could deliver such a large contract, knowing we simply had to. We won, and after the initial scramble, we thrived. This was the big break we needed and we have not looked back.

Twelve years later, MCIS has grown organically without any outside investment and is now a one-stop shop that offers 50 language services. Our main services comprise translation (including sight translation), face-to-face interpretation (consecutive and simultaneous), telephone interpretation (immediate and scheduled), video interpretation, CART and transcription services. It has been a long hard road going from 2.5 FTE to over 60 FTE, from 40 interpreters to over 6000 language professionals in 300 languages, including American Sign Language and Braille, from a handful of local community agency clients to over 800 customers in the broader public sector. More importantly, besides earning revenue to reinvest in public benefit projects, MCIS' work influences the lives of thousands across Canada, by giving a voice to those who are disenfranchised and training and work opportunities to thousands of bilingual immigrants and refugees.

What's next for MCIS and me?

MCIS is financial stable with several long-term contracts that will help us maintain our bottom-line. We are consolidating our pan Canadian presence and looking to grow globally. We are focusing on bringing 3 new services to market every year and will continue to offer bundled solutions. We will continue to build our global talent pool and partnerships with Language Service Providers and technology companies around the world.

We see tremendous potential to grow our one of a kind online Translator Training program both to earn revenue and to engage in humanitarian projects with organisations such as Translators Without Borders which are in disaster and high conflict zones, where "just in time" translations saves lives.

We will continue our advocacy advancing the importance of multilingualism to establish Canada's brand as the global society that the world can emulate. We never lose sight of the fact that our business strategy must align with our social impact objectives where we engage partners with advocacy initiatives and build the type of organizational culture and capacity that will support all of our efforts. Through our growth as a fiscally viable organization, we want to provide language solutions that significantly improve access to critical information and services supporting the rights, safety and well-being of people, and develop advocacy efforts focused on the promotion of language access as a basic human right.

In case you are curious, Canada did wonders for my husband's career. He rose to a rarefied role managing nuclear reactors. Our daughter made the most of Canada to develop her passion for the outdoors and after an Ivy League education lives an active and socially conscious life as a Management professional in London, England. As for me, I did not have a grand plan when I started out. In retrospect, my career blended together my passion for social justice with my education and experience. I could not have done as well if I had scripted it. If I did one thing right it was to approach life with wonder and curiosity, allowing experiences to unfold rather than try to control outcomes. Even today I come in to work grateful for the opportunity. I am equally comfortable handing it over to the next generation of leaders whom we are now in the process of preparing to step into my role. I will know it when the time is right for me to step down. I continue to intensify my practice of yoga and next on the cards is an intense Yoga Teacher Training Program and more time to introspect and just be.

Latha Sukumar, M.A. LL.B | Bio

2010 - National Award from the Women's Legal Education and Action Fund for being one of 15 lawyers in Canada who has advanced the equality rights of women.

2018 - Law and Entrepreneurship in the City of Toronto from a woman's organisation Dancing Damsels (http://www.ddshows.com/)

2018 - Women's Empowerment Award from the Mayor of Markham and Social Services Network, Markham.

An advocate for the rights of new comers, Latha has served on a number of community boards and has spoken in the media, before legislative committees and at public gatherings on victim rights issues. Latha believes in applying new discoveries she makes, to her personal and professional life and work and loves collaborative work and partnership building while participating in entrepreneurial opportunities. Besides being a social entrepreneur, Latha is an avid blogger, a yoga teacher and Vipassana meditator.

Executive Director, MCIS Language Solutions

September 1996 – Present , Toronto, Canada

Has led the transformation of MCIS Language Solutions (MCIS) into a social enterprise that engages local talent to provide a full suite of language services globally.

About MCIS

MCIS' greatest achievement has been its transformation from a small Scarborough based non profit, wholly dependent on government funding, providing interpretation services in 25 languages to a pan Canadian language solutions company which generates revenue through a commercial business enterprise to invest in its social impact initiatives and advance the cause of improving linguistic access for all. MCIS is now a one-stop shop that offers over 50 language services. Our main services comprise translation (including sight translation), face-to-face interpretation (consecutive and simultaneous), telephone interpretation (immediate and scheduled), video interpretation, CART and transcription services.

We offer services in over 300 languages including ASL, Braille, and Indigenous languages. We serve over 800 organisations in the Canadian public sector and are rapidly deploying technology to participate in the global market to serve all industries. Over the last 15 years we have trained over 6000 language professionals in Ontario through our pioneering online training programs for language professionals, giving them a means to earn a livelihood or at the very least to gain entry into the local job market. MCIS' achievement is particularly remarkable because we were dependent on year to year funding and, as a non-profit, had to grow organically without any outside investment. Also the global language industry consists of companies ranging in size from the very small to the very large private equities that invest heavily in technology which helps them drive down prices and therefore presents stiff competition for MCIS.

The language industry uniquely faces the challenges of technology disruption brought on by google translate, remote interpretation and other forms of automation that challenge traditional models of service delivery. It has therefore been a long hard road going from 2.5 FTE to over 60 FTE, from 40 interpreters to over 6000 language professionals, from a handful of local community agency clients to over 800 customers in the broader public sector including governments across Canada and from a budget of $150,000 to about $10 MM in the upcoming fiscal year. Two years ago, following a competitive bidding process, the Federal Government awarded MCIS a $3MM contract to provide interpretation services for the 25000 refugees we welcomed to Canada. This was not only a vote of confidence on the government's part but an opportunity for MCIS to participate in a project that totally aligned with our vision, mission and values. MCIS stays competitive by keeping costs down, by offering a solutions based approach, by establishing niche markets offering bilingual services, which require high levels of security clearance and with high quality customer service.

MCIS also has a Social Innovation Lab to find new ways to build partnerships and skills, to stay ahead of the curve with globalisation. Last year we organised a hackathon, MigrahackTO and an (Un)conference on Hacking the language industry. Other social impact projects included a recipe book called "*Food for Language*" created to raise money for a community kitchen for ex residents of Sandgate Women's Shelter, Documentaries for Change which involved screening documentaries in community settings to mobilise for social change and developing the Online Training to Address Human Trafficking for the Ministry of the Attorney General, which has been taken by over 2000 Ontarians to date.

York University - Osgoode Hall Law School

LL.B., Law, 1991 – 1994

York University

M.A., Social Psychology, 1988 – 1990

lathasukumar.com

@lathamcis

Latha Sukumar

www.mcislanguages.com

CHAPTER 7

IT'S NOT ABOUT ME: Success, Powered By God

By Chad Burmeister

You have 86,400 seconds in a day, and what you choose to do with those seconds count! **(Hint: If you don't have the time to read this chapter, skip to the last part of this chapter titled "*it's not about me*")**.

This has been my mantra since my early 20's and has given me the grit to consistently over-achieve expectations. On my LinkedIn page you'll find the phrase: "*Others describe me as high energy, high integrity and has an extremely high ability to execute*."

But it didn't start out this way…

In 1995, when I graduated from Colorado State University, my first job was with a company called Olsten Staffing Services. The interview was with an on-campus recruiter at CSU, and once I was hired, they flew me to New York City for a few weeks for training, then I relocated from Colorado to Arizona, jumped in the car from my new apartment and off to the new office!

Rewind the tape a second – because this part of the story is important – you see in New York City at

Olsten's new hire training, I utterly failed the role play. Although I was always a super-competitive youngster (rope climb in elementary school, soccer, kick-ball, swimming, and other sports), I was also an introvert – and in the 90's introverts stuck out like a sore thumb, because the internet wasn't invented by Al Gore yet!

***Recent Facebook post by my elementary school gym teacher, Mr. Tim Trelfa. He once shared with me at our church after I graduated from Willow Creek Elementary School, that I owned the fastest rope climb time for all grades for several years after graduating.**

Climbing a rope with ease didn't help me in New York City when the expectation of new hires was to learn the art of selling, and then master a role-play at the end of the class, in front of your peers! (It was the "*in front of your peers*" part that killed me, I utterly failed the role play, and flew home to Arizona with my tail between my legs wondering "*is sales for me*"?). But I apparently had the "*look*" because I was asked to be in a photo that made the back of the recruiting brochure for other college graduates!

Not only did I have the "*look*" of a sales professional, but I also submitted a "*sales hack*" to Selling Power Magazine that ended up getting published in the November/December 1998 edition, when the print edition was still distributed to thousands of sales people and sales leaders around the globe! The sales tip was called "*Cash in on Calling Cards*" and outlined how I would send along a calling card to prospects, and ask for a 15 minute meeting with them to learn about their business – and tell them about ours.

This "*invention*" didn't matter, because no matter how many meetings I booked, my introvert personality seemed to hold me back from cracking the code of becoming a successful sales professional.

After taking a month "*off*" after being fired from Olsten, I was fortunate enough to interview for Airborne Express – the air express carrier. And this time, I was laser focused on doing well in the 3-week sales training school in Seattle, Washington, and overall I did ok. Within 6 months of completing sales training, I became the #1 sales professional at Airborne Express – by selling a very large deal to U-Haul, that helped them ship license plate tags out to their fleet of trucks. Although Airborne was "*more expensive*" the value of getting the plates to the trucks on time, was worth more than the "*cost*" of the shipping charges. This deal taught me a lot about value.

From there, Steve Lapour, a colleague at Airborne Express was recruited to work for FedEx in Southern California. Within a few months, I joined him, and picked up and moved from Arizona to El Segundo, California (the neighboring city to Manhattan Beach where I would meet my wife, and best friend, Tracey Ellen Burmeister). I'll never forget the interview when Donna asked me question #25, sell me this pen (straight out of Wolf on Wall Street, but 20 years ago!).

The background of this moment – Phillip Ragatz was the hiring District Sales Manager (or DSM), and Kristi and Donna were there to interview as a panel. The sun was setting over LAX Airport, which is where the FedEx office was located, and I felt like I aced the first 24 questions. Then Donna flipped me her pen, and the dreaded "*sell me this pen*" question came up. You see, during the Olsten role plays (when I write this I think of the "*witch trials*", it was that scary to me to be in front of peers), that was one of the questions where I utterly froze up. This time I was armed and dangerous because I had seen this one before.

I took a deep breath, smiled, thought about what I had learned from the experience at Olsten, and started asking some questions:

Question #1: Kristi, you have a pen, right?
Christy – right.

Question #2: Phillip, you also have a pen?
Phillip – right.

Question #3: Donna, I've noticed that during this panel interview that you have all been

taking notes on every single question, and I assume that is required for all interviews at FedEx?
Donna – yes, that's correct.

Question #4: Donna, do you have a pen?
Donna – nope.

Question #5: Donna, I understand that you are engaged and live on the beach, and with the sun going down right now, assume that you'd like to get home to your fiancée?
Donna – yep.

Question #6: Donna, before you can leave, it seems that you will need to fill out question #25 on your page, is that correct?
Donna – yep.

Question #7: Wanna buy a pen? Donna – how much? Chad – a nickel.
Donna – I don't have a nickel.

At this point, Phillip reached in his pocket, flipped me a quarter, and said "*keep the change*".

You see, at Airborne Express, we sold a "*lower cost*" model, where at FedEx, we sold value. And by asking questions to uncover the value of the pen to Donna, we were able to sign a deal without sharing any of the features of the pen. Most sales professionals think that the features of their product will sell a deal – when it's the advantages and benefits that sell the deal.

Over the next few years, I completed an MBA at Loyola Marymount University in Los Angeles, worked for a few companies where I finally tipped the scale to a six-figure income (Celarix, i2 Technologies, AMR Research, and Nexgenix), but found myself back in the challenge of trying to be an extrovert while living as an introvert.

This is when I met Dr. Tathagata Dasgupta, a Double PhD, who would become my business partner and co-founder of Tele-SalesForce.com (unrelated to SalesForce.com) in around 2004. We had a vision of providing outsourced business development, powered with agents in India (lower cost, higher outputs). We signed over 50 clients and grew the business to $448,000 in our best year—but I wasn't ready to be a sales leader, I hadn't learned the lessons of leadership. Shutting down Tele-SalesForce.com was a hard thing to do – I thought I'd be CEO forever, but the time wasn't right for me.

For the next decade, I learned from sales leaders like John Simon, Mitch Tarica, Brent Sapiro and Dave Berman at WebEx, MJ Shutte at Riverbed, Travis Patterson at IronKey, Ben Sullivan at ON24, then Chris Beall at ConnectAndSell and Faiza Hughell at RingCentral. Each of these sales leaders taught me different things about sales leadership from staffing, to management, to forecasting and more. But the most important lesson in sales (and business) leadership came from MJ Shutte. Gabe Larsen, VP of Growth at InsideSales.com asked me for a quote on leadership for a blog he was writing recently, this is what I shared with him:

"You know you are a great leader when your team would walk through fire for you".

— MJ Shutte, my mentor a decade ago

"After ten years, I would still walk through fire for MJ Shutte, and several people I know would do the same for me!"

— Chad Burmeister

On December 1st, 2017, I resigned from a company where I was VP of Inside Sales, to join the company that I helped my co-founder start a few months earlier – ScaleX. And within 4 short months, have presented at multiple conferences including two AA-ISP Conferences (San Francisco and Chicago), two Sales 3.0 Conferences (San Francisco and Philadelphia), B2BMX in Scottsdale, Arizona, Frost & Sullivan in Lake Tahoe, Topo in San Francisco and we'll be attending Outbound in Atlanta, Unleash in San Diego, and the AI Summit in Chicago in the coming weeks. As of the writing of this chapter, in just 4 months, we've signed close to $1,000,000 in bookings, and will never look back.

Key findings into the top traits of the Top 5% vs. the Bottom 5% of sales professionals.

Dave Kurlan, CEO of Objective Management Group, contributed a chapter to Sales Hack, With Contributions From 25 of Greatest Sales Professionals of Our Time. Over the past decade, Objective Management Group has scored over 1M sales professionals to determine the common traits between the top 5% and the bottom 5% of sales professionals. Here are the findings.

Top 5%	Trait	Bottom 5%
99.5%	**Trainable and Coachable**	**0%**
100%	**Strong Desire for Sales Success**	**0%**
95%	Strong Commitment to Sales Success	33%
94%	Don't Make Excuses for Results	20%
78%	Don't Need to be Liked by their Prospects	6%
59%	Don't Get Emotional	10%
98%	Comfortable Talking about Finances	2%
79%	Supportive Sales Beliefs	0%
76%	Supportive Buying Habits	8%
96%	Sales DNA of 80 or Better	0%
95%	Rejection Proof	18%
100%	**Have Personal Written Goals**	**16%**
95%	High Money Tolerance (choking point)	35%
88%	Make Decisions to Buy without Thinking it Over	18%
77%	% of the Attributes of a Hunter	31%
45%	% of the Attributes of a Closer	8%
59%	% of the Attributes of a Qualifier	11%

***From the book Sales Hack, contributed by Dave Kurlan, CEO of Objective Management Group**

The #1 trait of the top 5% of sales professionals (when looking across over 1M sales professionals) is that they have a "*Strong Desire for Sales Success*".

How does this apply to my sales career: To illustrate, consider that as a freshman high school, I was the worst foosball player at the arcade. Over 4 years, and hundreds of games, I became "*ok*". In college, I bought a Tornado brand foosball table, watched several videos of how to shoot and strategy of the game, and after thousands of games and hundreds of hours of playing, I became one of the best players. Similarly, as described earlier in the chapter, I was fired from my first sales job. Why? Because I was a "*freshman*" in the sales game. After hundreds/thousands of hours of study, practice, and live sales calls, I can now say that I have earned the title of AA-ISP Top 25 Inside Sales Professionals in the country for eight of the past nine years (2010 – 2018).

The #2 trait of the top 5% of sellers, "*Have Personal Written Goals*".

How does this apply to my sales career: In the 1990's my Mom took me to a Success Seminar with Zig Ziglar, Peter Lowe, Tom Hopkins and more. One of the motivational speakers talked about the importance of having written goals. From that day forward, almost every year I would write down my one-year, two-year, five-year, and ten-year goals. I still have the scribbled on one-pagers in a file in my desk – and I've achieved every single goal from the amount of money I want to make, to starting a family, and more... the only goal that I have yet to achieve is owning a boat.

The # 3 trait of the top 5% of sellers, "*Trainable and Coachable*".

How does this apply to my sales career: Early in my career, I was a sponge. If you knew something that I didn't whether you were a CEO, VP of Sales, Sales Rep, or the front desk administrator, I didn't care, I wanted to learn and grow. In my most recent OMG assessment, I scored a 50% score in this category. What it reminds me is that I am now having a tendency to "*know the answer*" and sometimes that's not always a good thing.

The Objective Management Group Sales Assessment changed the way that I hire sales professionals, and how I assess my own strengths and weaknesses. Remember that if you have a "*Strong Desire for Sales Success*" and "*Have Personal Written Goals*", and are "*Trainable and Coachable*", you have exactly what it takes to start your Journey to Success!

"It's Not About Me"

"*It's not about me,*" are the first words of Pastor Rick Warren's book, The Purpose Driven Life, our church when we lived in Southern California in the early 2000's.

There have been many times throughout my career when I forget this sentence, and mantra, and attempt to put myself (me) first. When God sent his only son Jesus Christ who was crucified, died, and rose from the dead, he reminds us that it's truly not about "*me*".

When life seems to bring things to you that are insurmountable, these are some of the prayers and songs I've used to get through the tough times. (Side note: as I write this chapter, my family is going through one of these difficult times, and we are reminded of the prayers, and promises, of our Lord and Savior).

Prayer: "*I do and I ask God to help and guide me,*" was a phrase we learned in 8th grade confirmation class. I've said this out loud before Lacrosse games, interviews, and big sales calls. When we remember that God gave us our mind, body and spirit and he is here with us always, all things are possible, when we put our faith and trust in him

Prayer: When I pray the Lord's Prayer out loud, or in my mind, the sentence that I stress is "***thy will be done***". When I open myself to God's will, the most incredible things happen. As I shared with someone who was let go from his job, had a family of five, and was headed towards homelessness, when you pray to God, he answers 100% of the time. It might not always be the precise answer you were looking for, but it will be the "*right*" answer. This person is now a Director with his company, has two direct reports, and has thanked me multiple times for "*saving his life*". Thanks be to God!

Our Father, who art in heaven,
hallowed be thy Name,
thy kingdom come,
thy will be done,
on earth as it is in heaven.

Give us this day our daily bread.
And forgive us our trespasses,
as we forgive those
who trespass against us.

And lead us not into temptation,

but deliver us from evil.

For thine is the kingdom,
and the power, and the glory,
for ever and ever. Amen.

A verse from: Danny Gokey's - Masterpiece

You're making a masterpiece
You shaping the soul in me
You're moving where I can't see
And all I am is in your hands
You're taking me all apart
Like it was your plan from the start
To finish your work of art for all to see you're
making a masterpiece

What is Success?

The thesaurus provides synonyms for success including:

accomplishment	prosperity	eminence	snap	good luck
achievement	realization	fortune	strike	good times
advance	triumph	fruition	successfulness	grand slam
benefit	victory	hit	walkaway	gravy train
boom	win	killing	walkover	happy days
fame	arrival	laugher	bed of roses	lap of luxury
gain	ascendancy	maturation	big hit	éclat
happiness	attainment	reward	do well	
profit	clover	savvy	easy street	
progress	consummation	sensation	flying colors	

What then is the "*Journey to Success?*"

In my opinion, the journey to success is the pursuit of happiness, and opening up yourself to God's will for your life. It is taking a minute to "*stop and smell the roses*". It is helping other people to become successful. It is seeing Tiger Woods shoot a hole-in-one in Golf, or doing your first helicopter ski trip, or traveling to Italy, France, or Paris, or being in the room to hear the borning cry of your newborn child... The phrase "*it's the journey, not the destination*", is so true. As I've often said, if you didn't have bad days, you can't have great ones. Enjoy them all, they are a gift from God.

A poem about my "*Journey to Success*":

My Journey to success started with my Mom and Dad,
The gift of God, was the best gift I could have ever had.

The Journey to success began in first grade,
Being #1 in the rope climb, all the friends I'd made.

Off to High School, in a brand new town,
Brought new friends, who to this day, I still see around.

In College, I played Lacrosse,
And always wore around my neck a gold cross.

After college, I moved around a lot,
From transportation to software, and now programming a "sales bot".

I'm in my forties, and I have a lot to love,
But it's the Journey to success, that is the gift from above.

As you decide what to do in life,
Pray about it often, you'll always do what's right.

Dear God, please help and guide our family towards your peace,
And thank you for your promise that you're making a masterpiece!

Tribute to Tom Cunningham:

Tom Cunningham was a resilience expert—a fitting career for someone who was more resilient than almost anyone I've ever known. Tom was diagnosed with Systemic Juvenile Rheumatoid Arthritis at age 5 which is by far the worst of the over 100 types of arthritis. Tom had 4 hips, 4 knees, and 2 shoulders replaced. He was hospitalized more than 40 times. Yet, despite Tom's physical challenges, he ALWAYS answered AMAZING when asked how he was doing. Tom made more than 250,000 B2B telephone cold calls to Entrepreneurs, Presidents and C Level Executives during his 25+ year inside sales career. He shared the stage with Jim Rohn, Mark Victor Hansen (Chicken Soup for the Soul books), Deepak Chopra, Jeffrey Gitomer, Bob Burg, Dave Liniger (Founder of ReMax), Don Green, Frank Shankwitz, and many others.

I've had the honor of meeting a handful of people who have had various "*disabilities*" like Tom. Jake Olson, for example, USC's blind long-snapper. He has a similar outlook on life that Tom had – when he spoke at our office in 2017, just a few weeks after his first snap in a USC game. When asked about his outlook on life, he said he likely would not have had a scholarship to USC if he didn't go blind – although he'd probably prefer to have sight, you have to do what you can with what you are given.

Another person whose career was turned upside down was Danny Gans – known as the Man of Many Voices – who sold over $200M in box office tickets over his 13 years in Vegas. Danny blew out his knee shortly after achieving his dream of becoming a professional baseball player. Then he met someone at the hospital who shared a similar story of how he was able to pivot his life to do good, and long story short, Danny Gans become one of the most well-known people in Vegas for a decade.

Whether you are born with one of the worst diseases you could get, you go blind in your teens, or you have a career ending knee injury, learn from Tom Cunningham, Jake Olson, and Danny Gans – no matter what the curve ball, no matter how dire your situation appears to be, it's your choice whether you will let your situation define you, or whether you will define your life and make a difference. #ChooseToMakeADifference.

Thank you Tom for giving all of yourself to make a difference in this world.

Chad Burmeister | Bio

Chad Burmeister is the Co-Founder and CEO of ScaleX.ai, the leader in Sales Acceleration as a Service, Powered by Artificial Intelligence.

The thing Chad most passionate about - equipping today's modern sales professional with AI-powered sales strategies and technologies to dominate their market!

Chad was the Founding Chapter President of the AA-ISP Silicon Valley Chapter and Colorado Chapter. Chad was voted Top 25 Most Influential Inside Sales Professional by the AA-ISP 8 years in a row (2010 - 2018). Chad has held sales leadership roles with companies including Cisco-WebEx, Riverbed Technology, ON24, ConnectAndSell, and RingCentral.

Others describe Chad as high energy, high integrity and has an extremely high ability to execute.

CHAPTER 8

Small Things Can Make Big Differences

By Gautam Nath

Success comes in many forms

A Prelude. ....

It was past midnight, the sky was pitch-dark, but the mountain peaks around me were capped in snow. From the cockpit of the cargo aircraft, I could see the beginnings of a valley as we were targeted to land at Bishkek airport, nestled in the Kyrgyz range. The Ethiopian crew could not speak or read Russian and the Russian navigator could speak only limited broken English.

Reading the airway maps that were in Russian, he said, go to 300, the pilot started moving his stick when the navigator hurriedly corrected himself in crude English with a Russian accent, noo! noo! Noot three huundred . . . three thouusand! Sweat popped off the pilot's brow as he hurriedly adjusted and he barked at his crew, "*Get that civilian (me) out of my cockpit*". (To be continued later in this chapter)

Welcome to this chapter of my travails – which shares how journeys of success enter our lives and how each experience makes us a better person.

Paradise on Earth

One country on earth where you cannot travel without a guide. One country on earth where there is no killing of animals nor fishing allowed. One country on Earth with the highest happiness index. One country on earth ruled by a king and his generation's forever. One country on earth that was never ruled by outsiders and so does not need to celebrate an independence day.

Bhutan, also known as the Switzerland of the east, was one journey of my life that helped open my eyes in learning how people lived so happily. Don't get me wrong, they eat lots of meat and fish but everything comes from India across the border. A visitor to the border towns in India will be amazed by the number of abattoirs set up there doing brisk business. The Bhutanese rivers abound with fish and only the King is allowed to fish there. This aspect of not killing anything makes Bhutan one of the most peaceful countries in the world with a crime rate close to zero.

Experiencing this over a two-week visit traveling with our guide Dorji, in a 1940's Plymouth, was mind-boggling. Driving high up in the Himalayan ranges, drinking water fresh from natural springs, being welcomed as guests into people's homes and being in touch with nature. This was truly a journey that informed of the wide spectrum of humanity on earth and the way different people live.

These experiences made me a better person - calmer, more reflective and more patient with challenges that come your way in life.

I recall trekking hours up a very steep narrow walkway to reach the Paro Taktsang Monastery nestled on a mountain peak. As we rested halfway, our guide Dorji told us that Prince Charles had traveled the same path two weeks ago and has rested at the same spot. Yes, strangely, I could sense royalty!

As I reached the peak, a group of young monks in their orange robes walked past when suddenly a cellphone rang and interestingly, the ring tone was a popular Bollywood theme song. Here we were, so many hundreds of miles away from the madding crowds, only to be greeted by this tune. Wow! Life shows you never know what to expect.

Thereafter, I visited a wildlife park high in the mountain and saw a herd of the most rare and wondrous animal called the Takin; body of a cow and head of a goat. Some interesting folklore goes behind this but that is another long story.

I also learned another interesting lesson of life. King Jigme Singye Wangchuk was married to 4 sisters. He had four palaces built and gave one to each sister so he could visit them separately. But then, he had his own majestic King's Palace, independent and exclusive for himself where he normally lived. That kept him a wise and happy man.

Interestingly, as we were young and wanted to party, Dorji took us to a basement in Thimphu, the capital city, later that night. This was just like a New York nightclub, booze was flowing, girls in miniskirts, latest western music, foreigners and locals mixing and everyone was friendly with each other. We made friends and partied till 4.00 a.m. in the morning. And I learned not to underestimate life's journeys and to always be prepared for learning something new.

A near Death experience (continued from Prelude)

Sweat popped off the pilot's brow as he hurriedly adjusted and he barked at his crew,

"Get that civilian (me) out of my cockpit"'.

I was moved into a small cabin behind the cockpit and we could feel the aircraft attempt to land. There were some flashes of light in the dark sky as the pilot focused on his landing.

After three attempts, we landed and soon taxied to a stop. The crew opened the aircraft door and we were 30 feet up off the ground and everything around us was just white fields of snow. Soon we saw lights in the distance and two army jeeps with an aircraft ladder vehicle pulled up. They attached the ladder and climbed up into the cockpit with their machine guns. They did not speak English and took our passports, our pilot and the Russian-speaking navigator. Then got back into the jeeps and drove off, leaving two soldiers with machine guns at the foot of the ladder.

I gathered my courage and went down to the soldiers with peace offerings of a bottle of Johnny Walker and a carton of Marlboro's. In my broken Russian I understood what they said, "*You have landed illegally and our KGB will come and decide what will be done with you.*" I had visions of rotting in a Kyrgyzstan prison, or having to tend goats for the rest of my life on a Kyrgyz mountainside, not the happiest place on Earth.

Then everything changed; 6 black limos with a dozen huge trucks drove up. They had a pretty young redhead with them, Tatiana, who was an interpreter. She told me that these were my buyers and they have cleared everything with the security and we should relax in the limos on the tarmac.

A cup of hot chocolate and some Yanni playing in the warm limo was in store while the labor quickly offloaded the aircraft.

In two hours they were done, we were handed over our passports and flew off landing back in New Delhi. All in all, an overnight adventure.

The next day, our buyers faxed us a clipping from their local newspaper – "*Last night, an unidentified aircraft flew over Kyrgyzstan airspace and our anti-aircraft guns almost shot them out of the sky*".

Life's lesson, never take anything for granted.

Travel brings perspectives

We decided to do something on our bucket list – Backpack through Europe.

Equipped ourselves with sleeping bags, camping gear and steel supported backpacks, we flew from New Delhi using London UK as our base camp. Our friend Christopher's mum, Bridgette lived there so we settled in taking only the essentials on our backs. The best budget option available was the Eurobus so we booked that for a month. Soon we were off on the first leg of our journey across the English Channel to Paris.

The ride on the ferry was magnificent and we felt the warm breeze of the English Channel on our faces as we hung around on the deck. It was our first trip into Europe and we were excited about what lay in store ahead. We laughed and joked with some of our fellow travelers as they envied our adventure ahead.

Early morning, we reached Paris and were greeted by Leticia who took us home for a scrumptious breakfast. Two years ago, Leticia had visited her aunt, our friend Laure who lived in India and we had made friends.

Our global adventure was beginning; satiated with croissants, marmalade, country sausages and fresh orange juice, we decided to take the Paris metro into the city. Soon we were walking down Champs Elysees imbibing the aura of this boulevard. There were hundreds of people going about their business and lots of tourists taking pictures and posing with the human statues on the street. One clown decided to adopt us and danced and performed acrobatics including an animated slow dance with my wife. For 5 Euros, we escaped his clutches and made our way to the Louvre. The Louvre was out of this world and takes about three days to do justice but we went through it in three hours.

It was summer and that day was summer solstice. Paris streets transformed into pedestrian walkways with street bands performing various genres of music. From jazz to rap to classic and tin bands, we were in for a wonderful treat. I recall walking into a cathedral where the choir was singing. One girl's voice was so epic that we got goose bumps on our arms. What an experience, truly transforming and building great life perspectives for us.

We left the next day for south of France to spend a few days in La Mouche, a small town near Bordeaux. Leticia's aunt, our friend Laure, had her family home there and she was visiting from India too.

Our eyes took in the rolling green of France's landscape, we listened to quaint French speaking passengers and one pretty lady even began to sing as the train moved on. Some people passed around Parisian breads and pastries and we felt the true warmth and hospitality of the French people.

Laure received us at the station and after hugs and kisses; we drove off into the woods. The French drive really fast and soon we were holding on to our ears should they not fly off. In 36 minutes, we reached the Cadier family home, a big villa in the forest. Rooms were named after different countries and decorated in that fashion. There was a China Room, an India room, a Turkish room and a Japanese room. Her parents had never traveled outside of France but wanted their children to appreciate the bigger world outside. And now the children having grown up were settled across the world. Another interesting lesson that we learnt.

There was a quaint outhouse with all the comforts of home yet independent of the big villa and just perfect for us so we settled in.

It was already evening and as tradition, wine bottles were opened. In France, and especially in the country, we found that there was an appropriate wine for breakfast, lunch and dinner and everything in between. Asparagus pickled in wine, beets pickled in wine, radish pickled in wine and we were surprised that there wasn't a kitchen sink pickled in wine.

Our days went quickly; we met the village folk, had a few meals with neighbors, drove out for a swim in the Atlantic and were soon saying farewell to France and on route to Spain.

Our bus arrived in Madrid in good time and we spent the day on the streets; watching people, eating paella, looking at street art and a high point was the visit to the Cathedral, La Almudena. Next day, early morning we were now on a train to Barcelona. The journey was out of this world and unlike the rolling green fields of France; we experienced high mountains and the Balearic Sea on either side of the tracks. It was a treat and opened our eyes to the varied topography of Europe and yet more to come.

Barcelona is quaint, the large number of human statues on the boulevard stood out giving the city a feel of being artistic and bohemian. After resting on a bench overlooking the Mediterranean, we grabbed a light lunch and we proceeded to the airport to catch a quick flight to Milan.

We landed at Milan and took a taxi to the bus station to catch our connection to Venice.

And that is where we were waylaid.

While we were sitting with our backpacks and belongings at the station, a group of Albanian women and children surrounded us and started saying something we could not understand. We were overwhelmed with what was happening and were not sure what they wanted. Then they became more aggressive and started tugging at our clothes and the little kids began to make loud noises. We had had enough and shouted in a loud voice, "GO AWAY AND LEAVE US ALONE" causing people to turn and see what was happening. Just as quick as they had showed up, the group suddenly vanished into thin air. We sat down relieved and then I checked inside my belt pouch. My wallet was missing, the zip apparently had been opened and smartly put back in place.

I got up and ran out into the street to see if I could locate any of them but none were in sight. I saw a policeman and managed to convey the loss of my wallet. People gathered and we were told that they were Albanian refugees up to no good and by now would have disappeared into their hiding places. Our beautiful European trip was suddenly marred. And we learned another lesson in life. Since then, I used a small lock on my pouch and we were fine for the rest of the trip. Luckily did not lose too much as our passports were kept separately and I had a habit of keeping minimal spending cash in the wallet.

The journey went on, we met some more friends in Venice, went on to Rome, then Austria, Germany and the Czech Republic. Prague was special as we met my grandmother (from my mom's side) who was 99 years old and spent a lovely evening with her. Also memorable in Prague was a visit to the Museum of Medieval Torture as well as a head banging evening at Europe's biggest nightclub, Karlovy Lazne. Onwards, we journeyed to Brussels and then back to base camp in England to spend two good relaxed days with Aunt Bridgette.

There were lots more eye opening experiences during our European journey but that is for another day.

The life of a hermit crab

This adventure lies in Ontario Canada before we immigrated here on a permanent basis.

One of my life philosophies is to prepare for things important for you.

For this reason, I visit the office of a potential employer before an interview date to understand the route and the lay of the land. That way on D Day, I can focus on the interview.

If we have guests for dinner and I am going to try a new recipe, I would prepare it one week in advance just to get any glitches out of the way. My friends know me as the fall back man, always prepared and always open to address change. And so was our move to Canada.

One evening, my wife and I were sitting at home in New Delhi, having a glass of wine and reflecting on things. I was in my early 40's, on the corporate Board of Director's and she was with one of the best schools in the city. But we were restless; we had traveled the world but we were still restless. Were we going to be doing this for the rest of our life we wondered? And so I said, 'If we could live in any country in the world where would that be?" And we decided on two criteria – the developed world and an English speaking country.

Our shortlist yielded - US, UK, Canada and Australia.

Long story short, Canada came on top and literally after 5 ½ years of patience; we landed as immigrants and today are proud Canadian citizens. No dream is impossible, if you have the perseverance and patience to see it through.

So you must be thinking, where is the story here? Keep on reading................

In the 5 ½ years while we waited for our papers to be processed, we decided to pay a visit.

We landed at Pearson International airport and took a taxi to Bolton, Ontario where a 24 foot RV was waiting for us. 30 days later, we returned the RV and caught our flight from Pearson International airport back home then in New Delhi, India.

Come join our journey across Ontario living an adventure as a hermit crab.

In India we drive on the left, in Canada we drive on the right. In India an RV would be called a truck and it takes a special kind of person to drive trucks on the road. But we did it – with grit, determination, confidence and a silent prayer - anything is possible.

After having tanked up on provisions and gas, we were off to Algonquin Provincial Park. Algonquin is one of Ontario's largest nature parks with over 8,000 square kilometers of forest, 2400 lakes and 1200 kilometers of rivers - a true camping heaven.

For those who don't know, once you are driving an RV, you are in a different world. There is a separate RV road map of Ontario with the most scenic routes, identifying camping grounds across the province and with all do's and don'ts of safe RV travel.

We stopped for the night at a mid-way campground and soon learned all about hooking up for water and electricity and how to empty the dump.

As we were fresh of the plane, we decided to explore the RV camp. The air was so clean, we could smell steak being barbequed, and we were taking in the newness of Canada as our future home. Ahead of us, we saw a gaggle of geese, big ones and little ones and we said to ourselves, WOW! How cute, Canada is so close to nature. We walked closer to them to get a better glance at the little ones.

Suddenly everything changed, the big geese spread their wings and grew double in size and started the wildest ever honking. More than half a dozen of the big ones charged at us. You should have witnessed the funniest ever sight; two grown adults just off the plane from India being chased by a gaggle of Canadian geese down a Canadian boardwalk, frantically waving our hands in the air and running for our lives.

Welcome to Canada we thought as we caught our breath, things are not always the way they seem, eh!

Next day we reached Algonquin, and spent the next 2 weeks basking in the sun, swimming in the lakes, canoeing into the wild and hiking where no man has gone before. We alternated between park campgrounds experiencing nature, making friends and encountering animal sighting, near and far – Deer, Black bear, Moose, Beaver, Raccoon, Skunk and Porcupines.

To us at that time, Canada was a land full of natural beauty, deep blue lakes, plush green flora and fauna, abundance of food and drink and populated by the nicest of people. (A few years later we arrived in Toronto as landed immigrants and were walking the streets of Queen West, our home now. We could see the cracks on the sidewalks, the homeless on the streets, the paint peeling off walls and despair in people's eyes. Was this the same Canada?)

As a tourist and as a landed immigrant; your perspective takes on a different vision - that is the story of life.

We RV'd into North Bay and the west of the province imbibing Ontario's experiences and enjoying the benefits of RV travel. In some of the bigger towns, we would park on a vacant lot and catch a few hours of shut eye before moving on to our next camp destination. This experience is truly a bucket list item for those who have never. Today, am proud to call Canada home and can lie back, close my eyes and visualize the beauty of nature and the experiences of our travels. Very important to have this perspective in your strive towards success.

Taking a Break

Work life is tough, especially when you immigrate to a new country and do not have the network of family, friends, colleagues and relatives as back home.

Doctors, engineers, and other professionals are driving Uber's, or taking up non-meaningful survivor jobs to make ends meet. Often stress leads to abuse - substance, physical or mental.

Every individual needs to find a release; a release that allows expression of self - resulting in relief of stress. Some use yoga or meditation to unwind, reflect and to recharge.

I am a foodie. Food to me is an experience, a way of expression and a great stress buster. It also takes me away from the hustle and bustle of every day's hectic routine and gives me inner peace. Having a good meal is a pit stop in the rat race, a time to revive my energy, a time to reflect and a time to be thankful.

I started a foodies group several years ago on Facebook and we have close to 2200 members from

83 countries, split equally between sexes, largely in the 25 to 55 age band. We post photos of dishes, recipes, recommend places to eat and share food related knowledge. At last count, there are over 5000 photos and videos on the page. We are a large multicultural group sharing our passion and spreading happiness and peace across the world.

I end my chapter by bringing this a full circle.

If you have indeed survived to this point; you are on your journey to success. You are a real human being, capable of great things in your life, of loving others and of leaving behind a legacy. Be remembered for the good things you have done while you travel your journey of success.

May the force be with you!

A Tribute to Tom

Tom and I were LinkedIn connections for several years but never did our path cross. In early 2018, when I was thinking of writing a book, out of providence Tom reached out to me on LinkedIn.

He offered me an opportunity to be part of this Volume 9 in his series so we began a dialogue online. We had numerous back and forth conversations and I was always impressed with his prompt response and his passion and excitement about life.

In this short span of time, we grew into chat buddies such that I helped him in reaching out to my friends and bringing on other deserving authors, some are in this book.

Then lightning struck and we were all dumbfounded to hear that God needed him more up there and we had to do without. My first and last physical meeting with Tom was in visitation and that was truly sad.

He is remembered, and we all hope our few words in this Volume recognizes the value he brought to our lives and our journey ahead - Journeys of success in remembrance of you Tom!

Gautam Nath | Bio

Gautam Nath is a world traveler and a Canadian citizen with a multicultural background.

He is an experienced corporate marketing professional having worked for large global multinational blue chip companies such as Estee Lauder, S C Johnson and the Kantar group. His corporate experience spans both Canada and overseas. In Canada, he was Vice President – Strategy at one of the largest multicultural communications firms, Director at Environics Research and currently Principal at Multicultural Marketing Solutions Canada, a specialized consulting agency based in Toronto.

He has been passionate about giving back and was recognized as Canada's Top 25 immigrants in 2011. He serves on various Boards and advisory committees, speaks at institutions, agencies, universities and colleges and has appeared on various media platforms. Gautam mentors new Canadians and is also well known as a leading expert on multicultural marketing and diversity.

Gautam was recognized as Canada's Top 50 Board Diversity Professionals in 2017.

He was also honored with Ontario's highest, the June Callwood Outstanding Achievement Award for Voluntarism in 2017.

In 2018, he was further honored with Canada's highest, The Sovereign's Medal for Volunteers.

Gautam hosts a television series called Exploring Canada's Diversity and has been nominated to stand for the 2018 mayoral elections in the city of Toronto.

He is a '*must watch out for*' leader amongst Canada's diverse population and his passion for giving back is unrivalled.

"It is critical for our success as a nation that every individual learns and feels the passion of giving back to the community in one form or the other. You have to give back, that is the Canadian Way! These are journeys of success and exemplify the passion and energy that we bring from across the globe to our new home."

**(Canada's highest honor for volunteers,
The Sovereign's Medal)**

Napoleon Hill Bio

NAPOLEON HILL
(1883-1970)

"Whatever your mind can conceive and believe it can achieve."

— Napoleon Hill

American born Napoleon Hill is considered to have influenced more people into success than any other person in history. He has been perhaps the most influential man in the area of personal success technique development, primarily through his classic book Think and Grow Rich which has helped million of the people and has been important in the life of many successful people such as W. Clement Stone and Og Mandino.

Napoleon Hill was born into poverty in 1883 in a one-room cabin on the Pound River in Wise County, Virginia. At the age of 10 his mother died, and two years later his father remarried. He became a very rebellious boy, but grew up to be an incredible man. He began his writing career at age 13 as a "mountain reporter" for small town newspapers and went on to become America's most beloved motivational author. Fighting against all class of great disadvantages and pressures, he dedicated more than 25 years of his life to define the reasons by which so many people fail to achieve true financial success and happiness in their life.

During this time he achieved great success as an attorney and journalist. His early career as a reporter helped finance his way through law school. He was given an assignment to write a series of success stories of famous men, and his big break came when he was asked to interview steel-magnate Andrew Carnegie. Mr. Carnegie commissioned Hill to interview over 500 millionaires to find a success formula that could be used by the average person. These included Thomas Edison, Alexander Graham Bell, Henry Ford, Elmer Gates, Charles M. Schwab, Theodore Roosevelt, William Wrigley Jr, John Wanamaker, William Jennings Bryan, George Eastman, Woodrow Wilson, William H. Taft, John D. Rockefeller, F. W. Woolworth, Jennings Randolph, among others.

He became an advisor to Andrew Carnegie, and with Carnegie's help he formulated a philosophy of success, drawing on the thoughts and experience of a multitude of rags-to-riches tycoons. It took Hill over 20 years to produce his book, a classic in the Personal Development field called Think and Grow Rich. This book has sold over 7 million copies and has helped thousands achieve success. The secret to success is very simple but you'll have to read the book to find out what it is!

Napoleon Hill passed away in November 1970 after a long and successful career writing, teaching, and lecturing about the principles of success. His work stands as a monument to individual achievement and is the cornerstone of modern motivation. His book, Think and Grow Rich, is the all-time best seller in the field.

The Seventeen Principles

1. **Definiteness of Purpose**
2. **Mastermind Alliance**
3. **Applied Faith**
4. **Going the Extra Mile**
5. **Pleasing Personality**
6. **Personal Initiative**
7. **Positive Mental Attitude**
8. **Enthusiasm**
9. **Self-Discipline**
10. **Accurate Thinking**
11. **Controlled Attention**
12. **Teamwork**
13. **Learning from Adversity & Defeat**
14. **Creative Vision**
15. **Maintenance of Sound Health**
16. **Budgeting Time and Money**
17. **Cosmic Habitforce**

About John Westley Clayton

"You are who and what you create yourself to be"
—John Westley Clayton

Rock Star Maker, Bestselling Author, Publisher of Bestselling Books, Sales Trainer, Life Trainer, Life Mentor, Keynote Speaker... ROCK STAR!!!

John Westley Clayton is the publishing arm of the *Journeys To Success* series; and along with other multiple tiles to the John Westley Publishing brand, has come to represent quality within the industry.

Surviving a rough childhood, along with multiple setbacks, unbeknownst to John Westley, this fueled the fire for him to set out on his own and develop a pathway to success that fits his puritan work ethic. Through the years John Westley created a successful resume, outperforming in all areas of business, sales and management.

Through the years something started to awaken in him; only focusing on wealth development for years may have created physical comfort and freedom, but there was something missing. The pieces finally fell into place when he discovered *Think & Grow Rich* by Napoleon Hill.

Focusing on the prize of financial achievement alone wasn't enough; developing ones self as a well-rounded human being was the elusive secret John Westley had been looking for for years.

John Westley began manifesting a new reality and became a Napoleon Hill Certified Instructor, helping others achieve their goals.

As the CEO & Founder of John Westley Enterprises, John Westley has become the '*Rock Star Maker*' and the secret weapon behind many of today's thought leaders. Under his ***Rock Star*** *4 life* brand, he helps individuals build the life they want by stepping out of their comfort zone and onto a bigger stage. Providing group coaching, one-on-one mentoring, image and personal brand creation and publishing. John Westley's work brings Fortune 500 business solutions to a group of handpicked students.

For the past 10 years, he's been teaching entrepreneurs, educators, corporate leaders and people from all walks of life how to create the life they truly desire by making the choices that best serve them in their professional and personal lives.

Today, as a peak performance coach and personal development strategist, John Westley's programs have launched dozens of individuals into ROCK STAR status.

Got a dream? He'll place it center stage.

www.johnwestley.com

info@johnwestley.com

About Brad Szollose

Brad Szollose

(pronounced zol-us)

"...No one knows Millennials or cross-generational management better than Brad, and it shows; our attendees are still talking about his work."

— Robbins Research International, Inc., a Tony Robbins Company